STUART MCHARDY has lectured and written on many aspects of Scottish history and folklore both in Scotland and abroad. His life-long interest in all aspects of Scottish culture led to his becoming a founding member and president of the Pictish Arts Society. From 1993-98 he was also the Director of the Scots Language Resource Centre in Perth. Following many years on the seminal *McGregor's Gathering* (BBC Radio Scotland) he has continued to broadcast on radio and television. He lectures annually at Edinburgh University's Centre for Continuing Education in the areas of Scottish mythology, folklore and legend. He is also the author of a children's book, *The Wild Haggis and the Greetin-faced Nyaff* (Scottish Children's Press, 1995) and has had poetry in Scots and English published in many magazines. Born in Dundee, McHardy is a graduate of Edinburgh University and lives in that city today with his wife Sandra.

By the sam

The Pagan Symbols of the Picts (Luath Press Ltd, 2012)

New History of the Picts (Luath Press Ltd, 2010)

Luath Storyteller: Tales of the Picts (Luath Press Ltd, 2005)

MacPherson's Rant: And Other Tales of the Scottish Fiddle (Birlinn, 2004)

School of the Moon: The Highland Cattle-Raiding Tradition (Birlinn, 2004)

The Silver Chanter: And Other Piper Tales (Birlinn, 2004)

The Quest for the Nine Maidens (Luath Press Ltd, 2003)

The Quest for Arthur (Luath Press Ltd, 2001)

Scots Poems to be Read Aloud (Luath Press Ltd, 2001) introduced and compiled by Stuart McHardy

Edinburgh and Leith Pub Guide (Luath Press Ltd, 2000)

The Wild Haggis an the Greetin-faced Nyaff (Scottish Children's Press, 1995)

Tales of Whisky and Smuggling (House of Lochar, 1991)

Strange Stories of Ancient Scotland: Landmarks and Legends (Lang Syne Publishers, 1989)

On the Trail of Scotland's Myths and Legends

STUART McHARDY

Luath Press Limited

EDINBURGH

www.luath.co.uk

First Published as *Scotland: Myths, Legend and Folklore* 1999
Revised Edition 2005
Reprinted 2012
Reprinted 2013
Reprinted 2015
Reprinted 2016

The paper used in this book is recyclable.
It is made from low chlorine pulps produced in a low energy,
low emissions manner from renewable forests.

Printed and bound by
Bell & Bain Ltd., Glasgow

Maps by Jim Lewis

Illustrations by Nulsh the Bold, Scottish Cartoon Art Studio, Glasgow

Typeset in 10.5 point Sabon by
3btype.com

In Memoriam

Martin Hendry

1943–1999

Contents

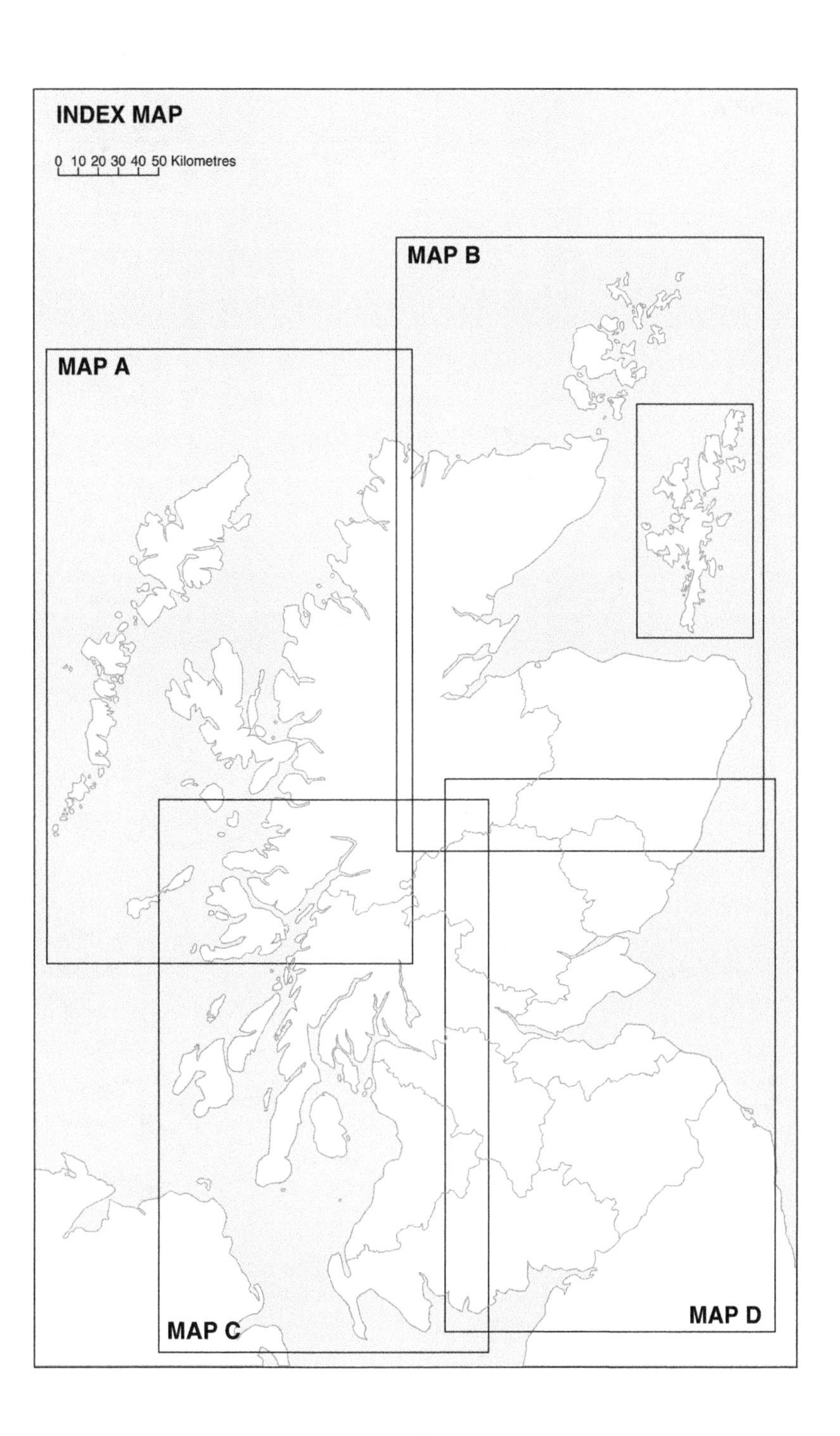
INDEX MAP
0 10 20 30 40 50 Kilometres
MAP A
MAP B
MAP C
MAP D

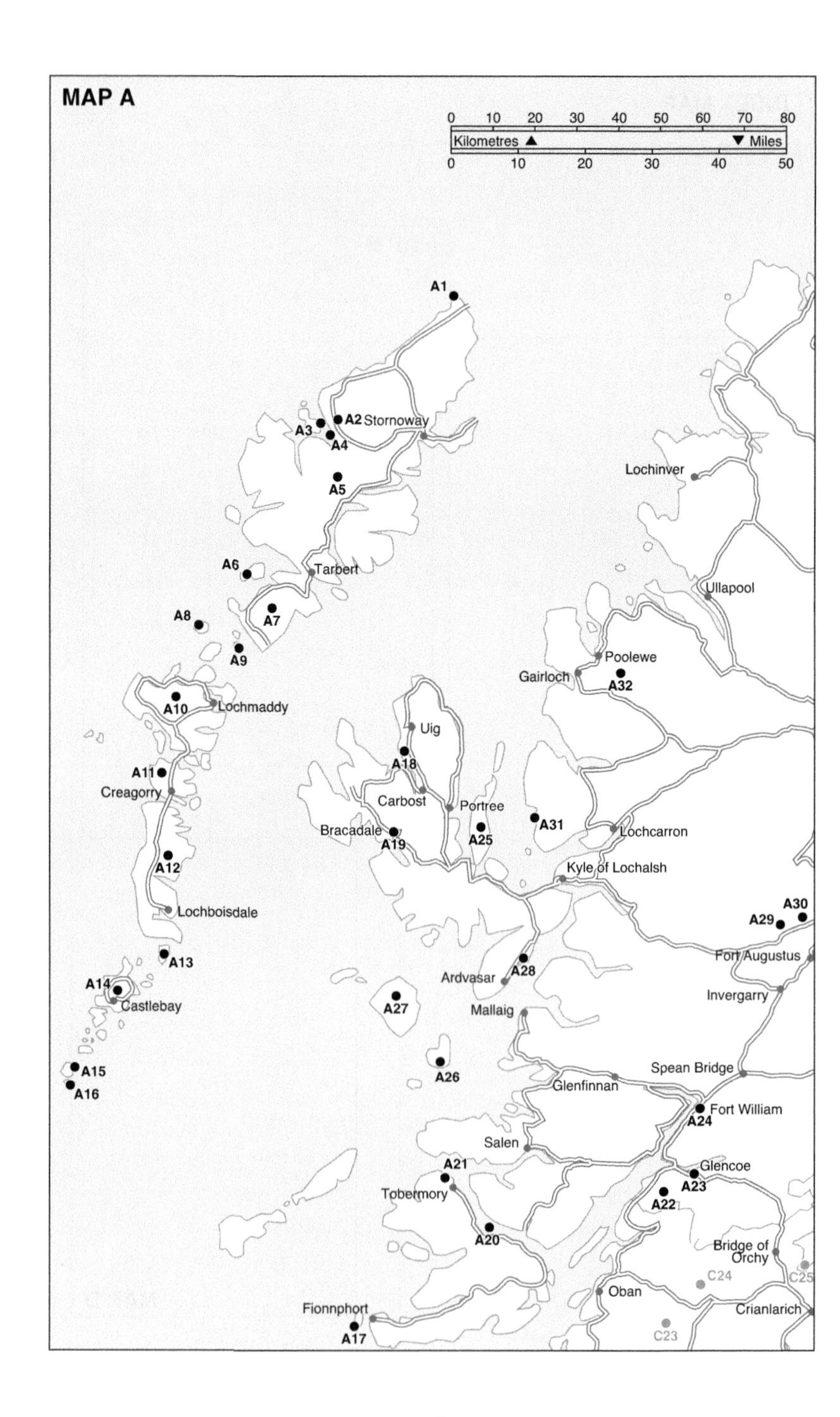

MAP A
Kilometres
Miles
0
10
20
30
40
50
60
70
80
0
10
20
30
40
50
A1
A2
Stornoway
A3
A4
A5
Lochinver
A6
Tarbert
Ullapool
A7
A8
A9
Poolewe
Gairloch
A32
A10
Lochmaddy
Uig
A18
A11
Creagorry
Carbost
Portree
Bracadale
A19
A25
A31
Lochcarron
A12
Kyle of Lochalsh
Lochboisdale
A30
A29
A13
Fort Augustus
A28
Ardvasar
A14
Castlebay
A27
Invergarry
Mallaig
A26
Spean Bridge
A15
A16
Glenfinnan
Fort William
A24
Salen
A21
Glencoe
A23
Tobermory
A22
A20
Bridge of Orchy
C24
C25
Oban
Fionnphort
Crianlarich
A17
C23

Key to Map A

Ref		Page
A1	Butt of Lewis: said to be formed from giant's head	100
A2	Breasclete: village by Calanais	113
A3	Loch Roag: loch from which magical cow appeared	111, 112
A4	Calanish: major standing stone alignment	105, 111, 112, 113, 132, 149
A5	Lewis: island where Calanais is situated	100, 105
A6	Taransay: island formed from giant's head	100
A7	Harris: said to be part nine-headed giant's body	100
A8	Pabbay: island formed from giant's head	100
A9	Killegray: island formed from giant's head	100
A10	North Uist: said to be part of giant's body	66
A11	Benbecula: said to be part of giant's body	100
A12	South Uist: said to be part of giant's body	100
A13	Eriskay: island formed from giant's head	100
A14	Barra: part of giant's body	100
A15	Mingualay: island formed from giant's head	100
A16	Sound of Bernera: island formed from giant's head	100
A17	Iona: important sacred centre	57
A18	Cuidrach: site of battle in Skye	48
A19	Bracadale: site of story of female kelpie	64
A20	Sound of Mull: site of hag's death	89
A21	Mull – Carn na Caillich: cairn named after hag	23
A22	Glen Duror: site of glaistig story	70
A23	Glencoe: site of Pap of Glencoe	20, 144
A24	Fort William: mentioned in tale of Serjeant Mor	32
A25	Raasay: mentioned in tale of nine-headed giant	54, 100
A26	Eigg: site of holy well	100, 120, 121
A27	Rum: mentioned as raided by nine-headed giant	100
A28	Loch nan Dubrachan: location of tale of Kelpie	64
A29	Dun Dreggan: hillfort where Finn killed a dragon	55
A30	Glenmoriston: site of story of St Merchard	54
A31	Applecross: ancient ecclesiastical site	54
A32	Loch Maree: site of pagan rites	55

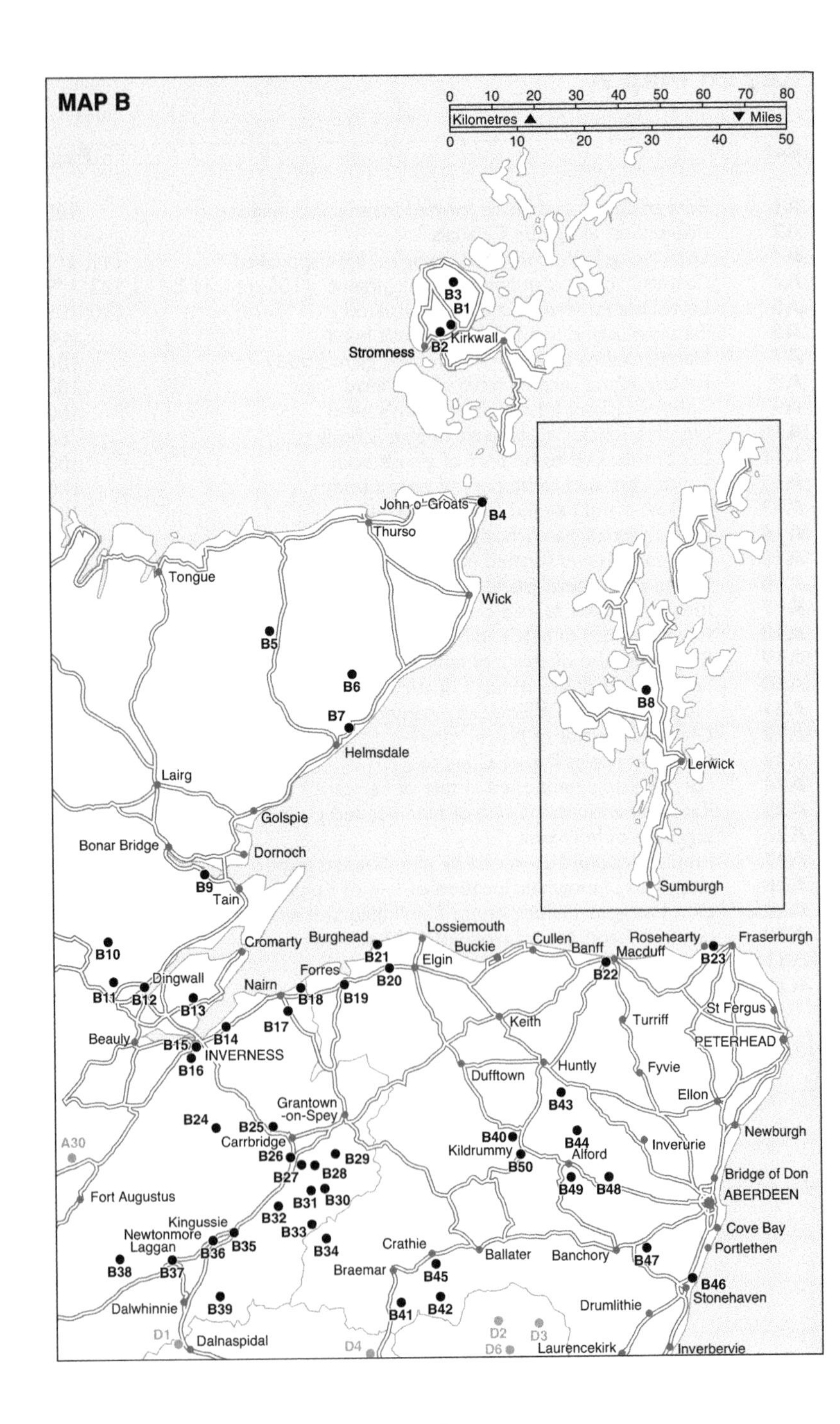
MAP B
Kilometres
Miles
Stromness
Kirkwall
B1
B2
B3
John o' Groats
B4
Thurso
Tongue
Wick
B5
B6
B7
Helmsdale
Lairg
Golspie
Bonar Bridge
Dornoch
B9
Tain
B8
Lerwick
Sumburgh
Cromarty
Burghead
Lossiemouth
Buckie
Cullen
Banff
Macduff
Rosehearty
Fraserburgh
B10
B11
B12
Dingwall
B13
Nairn
Forres
B18
B19
B20
B21
Elgin
B22
B23
St Fergus
Keith
Turriff
PETERHEAD
Beauly
B15
B14
B17
INVERNESS
B16
Dufftown
Huntly
Fyvie
Ellon
Grantown -on-Spey
B24
B25
Carrbridge
B43
Newburgh
B40
Kildrummy
B50
B44
Alford
Inverurie
B26
B27
B28
B29
Bridge of Don
ABERDEEN
B49
B48
A30
Fort Augustus
B31
B30
B32
Kingussie
Newtonmore
Laggan
B33
B35
B36
B34
Crathie
Cove Bay
Portlethen
Ballater
Banchory
B47
B38
B37
Braemar
B45
B46
Stonehaven
Dalwhinnie
B39
B41
B42
Drumlithie
D1
Dalnaspidal
D4
D2
D3
D6
Laurencekirk
Inverbervie

Key to Map B

Ref		Page
B1	Maes Howe: magnificent chambered tomb in Orkney	108, 149
B2	Stenness: major stone circle in Orkney	107
B3	Orkney: site of major megalithic remains	107, 108
B4	John o Groats: location of Silkie story	66
B5	Forsinard: site of giant story	101
B6	Maiden Pap: breast-shaped hill	20, 145
B7	Navidale: site of ancient sacred enclosure	124
B8	Shetland: location of fire festival	41
B9	Edderton: story of giant putting stones	94
B10	Ben Wyvis: story of the Cailleach	22, 134
B11	Strathpeffer: story of giants putting stones	109
B12	Dingwall: site of pagan practices	73
B13	Clootie Well: ancient healing well	4, 116, 136
B14	Culloden: site of another clootie well	117
B15	Inverness: location of Tomnahurich	119
B16	Tomnahurich: ancient sacred mound and cemetery	12, 13, 14, 125
B17	Auldearn: site of witch activities	72, 77
B18	Loch Loy: site of witch activities	77
B19	Forres: site of witch coven	72, 77
B20	Knock Of Alves: site of witch coven	72
B21	Burghead: site of midsummer fire festival	4, 41
B22	Banff: site of ancient fair	55
B23	Pitsligo: site of nine maidens well	115
B24	Strath Dearn: story of well moving to Canada	119
B25	Loch Slochd: site of kelpie story	62
B26	Granish Moor: location of prophesying witches	109
B27	Loch nan Carraigean: site of stone circle	109
B28	Loch Pityoulish: site of kelpie story	63
B29	Tullochgorm: location of brownie tale	68
B30	Loch Uaine: part of thieves' road	38
B31	Loch Morlich: part of thieves' road	38
B32	Loch an Eilean: part of thieves' road	39
B33	Lairig Ghru: pass through Cairngorms linked to Grey Man	102
B34	Ben Macdui: location of Grey Man of Ben Macdui	102
B35	Kingussie: mentioned in story of witch of Laggan	78
B36	Newtonmore: story of wizard eating serpent	79
B37	Laggan: location of witch of Laggan	78
B38	Dalarossie: sanctuary site witch failed to reach	79
B39	Gaick: home of hunter who fought witch of Laggan	78
B40	Tap o Noth: home of giant	95, 145
B41	Glen Clunie: possible birthplace of Cam Ruadh	34
B42	Lochnagar: site of breast-shaped peak	20, 134, 144, 145
B43	Maiden Stone: Pictish symbol stone with legend	84, 143
B44	Bennachie: breast-shaped peaks and site of several tales	20, 84, 85, 94, 95 96
B45	Balmoral: site of Shandy Dann ceremony at Halloween	47
B46	Stonehaven: location of midwinter fire festival	41
B47	Durris: location of midsummer fire festival	49
B48	Skene: home of Wizard Laird of Skene	81
B49	Tough: site of nine maidens well	115
B50	Kildrummy: site of nine maidens well	115

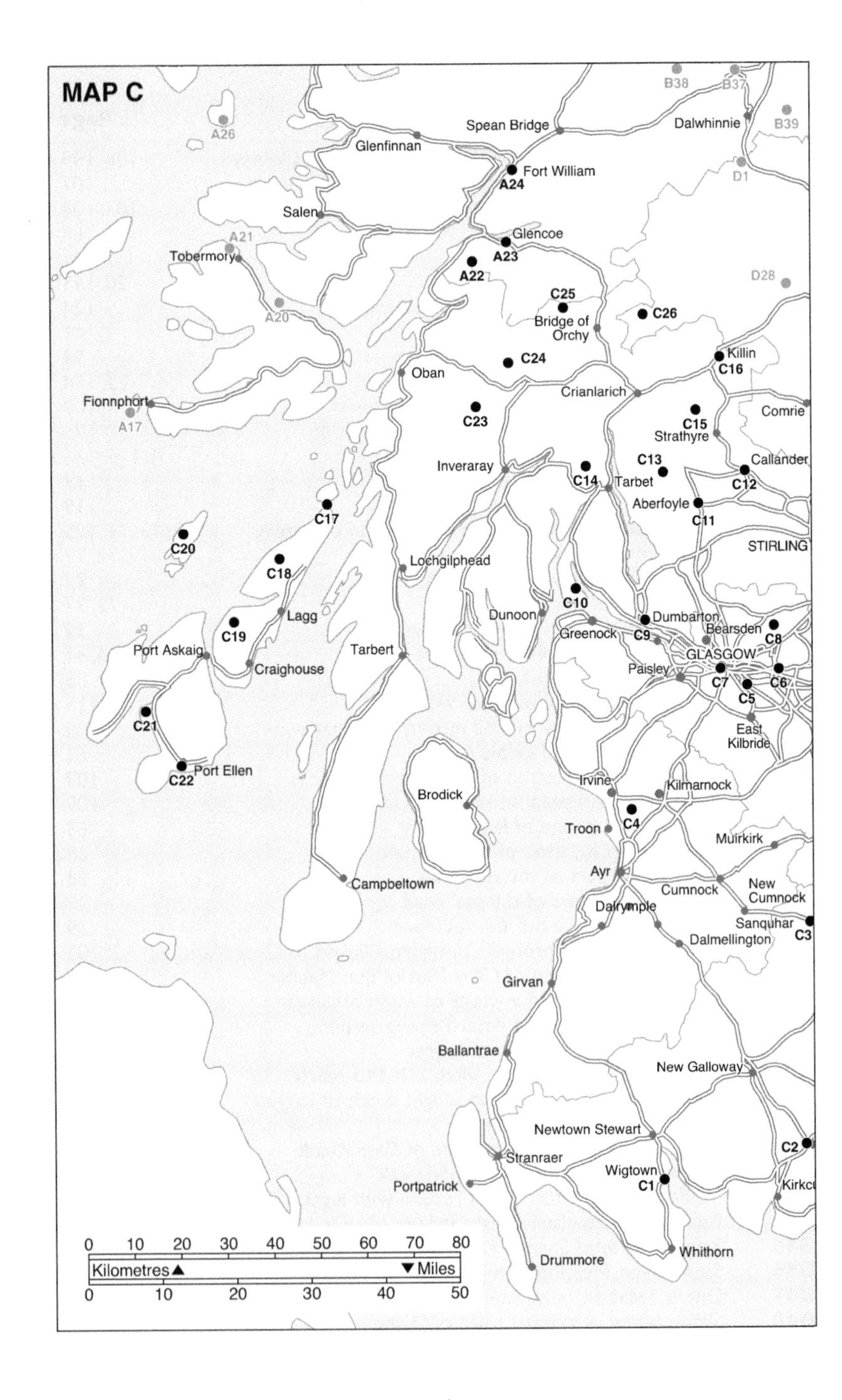
MAP C
A26
Spean Bridge
B38
B37
Dalwhinnie
B39
Glenfinnan
Fort William
A24
D1
Salen
A21
Glencoe
Tobermory
A23
A22
D28
C25
C26
A20
Bridge of Orchy
Killin
C24
C16
Oban
Crianlarich
Fionnphort
A17
C23
C15
Comrie
Strathyre
C13
Callander
Inveraray
C14
Tarbet
C12
Aberfoyle
C17
C11
C20
STIRLING
C18
Lochgilphead
C10
Lagg
Dunoon
Dumbarton
Bearsden
C19
Greenock
C9
C8
Port Askaig
Tarbert
GLASGOW
Craighouse
Paisley
C7
C6
C5
C21
East Kilbride
Port Ellen
C22
Irvine
Kilmarnock
Brodick
C4
Troon
Muirkirk
Ayr
Campbeltown
Cumnock
New Cumnock
Dalrymple
Sanquhar
C3
Dalmellington
Girvan
Ballantrae
New Galloway
Newtown Stewart
C2
Stranraer
Wigtown
C1
Portpatrick
Kirkc
Whithorn
Drummore
0 10 20 30 40 50 60 70 80
Kilometres
Miles
0 10 20 30 40 50

Key to Map C

Ref		Page
C1	Wigton: location of Bride's well	116
C2	Loch Carlingwark: site of ancient votive offerings	25
C3	Sanquhar: location of Bride's well	116, 143
C4	Dundonald: site of St Monenna dedication	118
C5	Rutherglen: location of Halloween baking ceremony	46
C6	Carntyne: probable site of fire festival	41
C7	Glasgow Cathedral: founded by St Kentigern	52
C8	Tintock: ancient fire site	41
C9	Dumbarton: site of St Monenna dedication	118
C10	Roseneath: site of ancient sacred grove	124
C11	Aberfoyle: site of fairy hill and disappeared minister	16
C12	Callander: story of Beltane rites	43
C13	Ben Venue: meeting place of forest spirits	67
C14	Ben Arthur: Arthurian placename	89
C15	Balquhidder: location of Beltane rites	42
C16	Killin: location of Beltane rites	42
C17	Corryvreckan: great whirlpool linking goddess and Columba	21, 138, 147
C18	Jura: island south of Corryvreckan	21
C19	Paps of Jura: breast-shaped peaks	20, 134, 141, 144
C20	Colonsay: site of story of moving well	118, 119
C21	Finlaggan: site of story of moving well	119
C22	Port Ellen: story of princess and frog	119
C23	Kilchrennan: location of 'two hunchbacks' story	17
C24	Ben Cruachan: mountain associated with Cailleach	22, 134, 135
C25	Rannoch Moor: hideout of post-Culloden Cateran	30, 31
C26	Rannoch Moor: The Cailleach's House	137

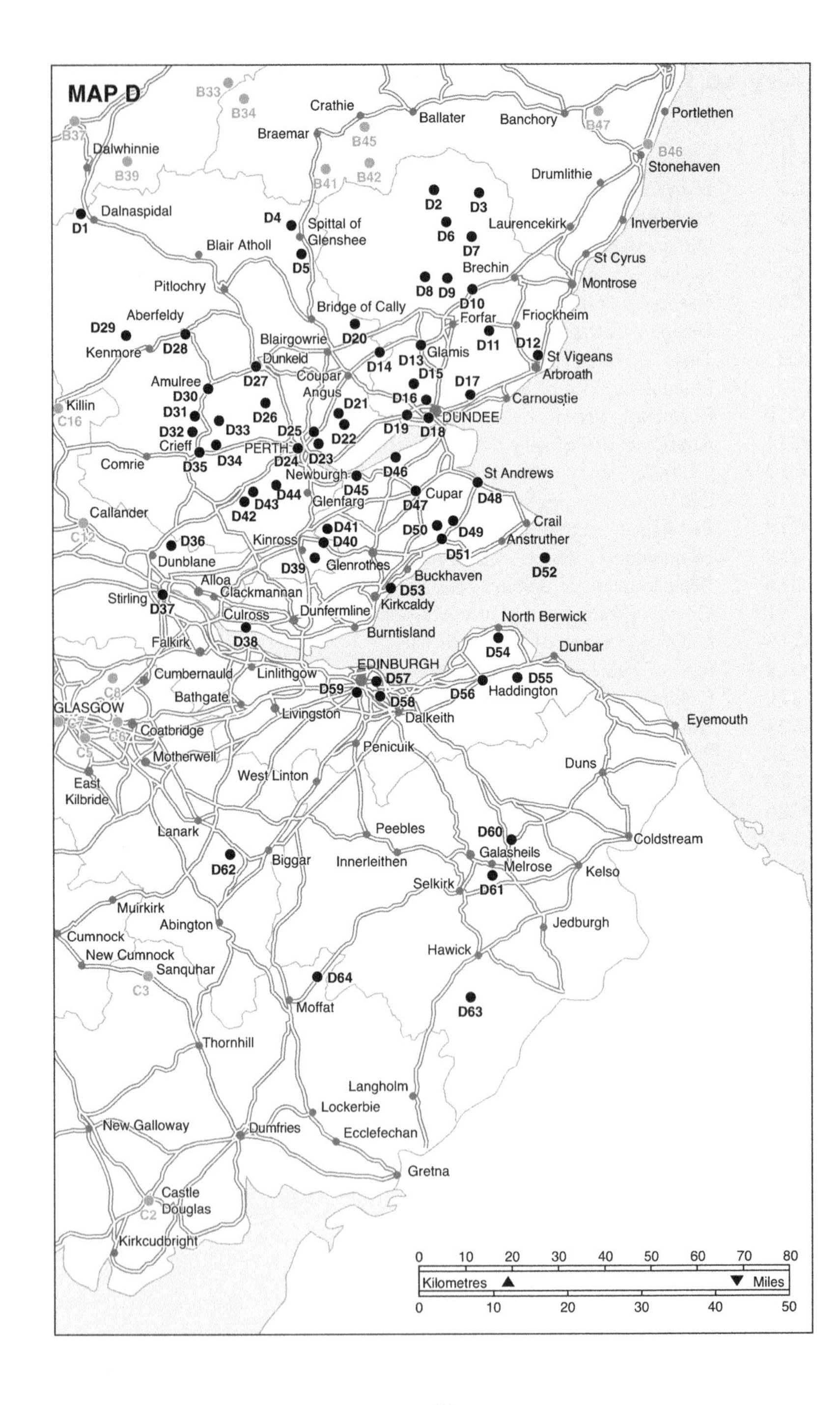
MAP D
B33
B34
B37
Crathie
Ballater
Banchory
Portlethen
B47
Braemar
B45
Dalwhinnie
B46
Stonehaven
B39
B41
B42
Drumlithie
D2
D3
Dalnaspidal
D1
D4
Spittal of Glenshee
D6
Laurencekirk
Inverbervie
D7
Blair Atholl
D5
St Cyrus
Brechin
D8
D9
Montrose
Pitlochry
D10
Bridge of Cally
Forfar
Friockheim
Aberfeldy
D29
D20
D11
D12
Kenmore
D28
Blairgowrie
Glamis
St Vigeans
Dunkeld
D14
D13
D27
Coupar Angus
D15
Arbroath
Amulree
D17
D30
D21
D16
Carnoustie
Killin
C16
D31
D26
D19
DUNDEE
D32
D33
D25
D22
D18
Crieff
PERTH
D34
D24
D23
Comrie
D35
D46
Newburgh
St Andrews
D45
D44
Cupar
Glenfarg
D48
D43
D47
Callander
D42
Crail
D41
D50
D49
C12
D36
Kinross
D40
Anstruther
D51
Dunblane
D39
Glenrothes
D52
Alloa
Buckhaven
Clackmannan
D53
Stirling
D37
Kirkcaldy
Culross
Dunfermline
North Berwick
Burntisland
D38
Falkirk
D54
Dunbar
EDINBURGH
Cumbernauld
Linlithgow
D57
D55
C8
D59
D56
Haddington
Bathgate
D58
GLASGOW
Livingston
C7
Dalkeith
Eyemouth
Coatbridge
C6
C5
Penicuik
Motherwell
Duns
East Kilbride
West Linton
Peebles
D60
Lanark
Coldstream
Galasheils
D62
Melrose
Biggar
Innerleithen
Kelso
Selkirk
D61
Muirkirk
Jedburgh
Abington
Cumnock
Hawick
New Cumnock
Sanquhar
D64
C3
D63
Moffat
Thornhill
Langholm
Lockerbie
New Galloway
Dumfries
Ecclefechan
Gretna
Castle Douglas
C2
Kirkcudbright
0
10
20
30
40
50
60
70
80
Kilometres
Miles
0
10
20
30
40
50

Key to Map D

Preface

AS A CHILD TOURING SCOTLAND I constantly nagged my parents to visit stone circles, brochs and standing stones. As I grew older I began to realise that many of these ancient sites had stories told of them and I found these stories as entrancing as the sites themselves. Tales were originally handed down through the generations by word of mouth, in Gaelic, Norse or Scots. They survived because they had meaning for both the people telling them and the people listening to them. Before writing this was how all human knowledge was transmitted; tales and legends were of central importance to human society. If they had no significance they would not have survived long enough to have been written down. For many years I have been researching Scottish legend and folklore and though there is much in common with the lore of other countries like England, Ireland, Scandinavia and Wales, our culture is uniquely our own.

I have spent much of my life researching Scotland's past to try and gain a clearer understanding of who I am. What I have found is that Scotland is not a Celtic country, but a Scottish country in which traditions and beliefs often called 'Celtic' are just as rooted in the traditions of Germanic-speaking peoples, like the Scandinavians, the English, and of course Scots speakers. The old phrase 'We're aw Jock Tamson's bairns' perhaps deserves a postscript: we're aw mongrels as weel. The traditions and tales in this book are intended to illustrate the diversity and complexity of Scottish culture.

Scotland's landscape is renowned for its beauty and visitors flock here from all over the world despite our often atrocious weather. I hope these stories show that our landscape is not just rich in beauty but also rich in lore and legend created over thousands of years. As we enter a new and potentially exciting political situation it is important that we try and get as clear a picture as we can of who we are and where we come from.

Stuart McHardy

Introduction

People come from all over the world to visit Scotland. Its beauty is well known – the magnificent mountains, the lonely glens and lush straths, tumbling rivers and placid lochs – all can touch the heart and stir the soul.

For all the vastness of the Scottish landscape, each of its mountains has a particular story connected to it. From the dawn of time, the myths and legends of Scotland and the exploits of those who lived here have come down to us in stories in Gaelic and Scots, tales from times when those languages themselves had yet to breathe.

Writing came to Europe only a few thousand years ago and much of the material in this book comes from before then. People then loved their land even more than we do today: they saw themselves as tied to it in ways modern city-dwellers have long forgotten. Much of the material in this book comes directly from those ancient times, reworkings of the great themes of life and death, love and liberty, told against the background of the Scottish landscape. It was and is a landscape of the eye, the heart and the soul of the peoples who have lived here. Magical animals, supernatural beings, heroes, giants and goddesses walk this landscape. As the ancient art of storytelling bursts into new flower, many of these tales are being told again as they once were.

Many things have changed over the past centuries – languages, religions, technology – but the love of the land survives, the glory in its splendour which informs the substance of its legends. What they tell us above all is that we are not so different from our far-off ancestors, and perhaps in the face of environmental destruction and world-wide pollution we may yet learn from them how to live in better harmony with the earth.

The past few decades have seen a world-wide resurgence of people wanting to know more about their 'roots', especially in Europe. Although there are varying reactions all over the world to this situation, here in Scotland we have our own way of doing things. There is a growing interest and participation in the rituals surrounding such ancient sites as the Clootie Well (B13) on the Black Isle, north of Inverness. This ancient sacred well is now a well-known tourist spot and people come from great distances to tie a rag to the trees adjoining the well and to make their wish. This is simply the continuation of an old tradition, once extremely widespread. In this book we shall look at some of the sites and rituals associated with this kind of ancient well-worship.

But there are examples of rituals practised even in Scotland's cities today. Calton Hill (D57) in Edinburgh – itself a name redolent of ancient belief – is the traditional site for a Beltane fire ceremony which has just been revived. It is now attended by thousands as dusk falls on the 31 April (following the traditional way of counting the new day from when the old one dies). This fire festival once took place all over Britain, a rite of sanctity and fertility. Though the actual ceremony today owes more to Mediterranean influences than traditional Scottish behaviour, the celebration and the use of fire, ritual dance and music all echo the May Day rites that seem to have come from the dawn of time. Other parts of Scotland too have seen their own Beltane fires lit, and other fire festivals such as the Burnin o the Clavie at Burghead (B21) or the Up-Hellya Festival in Shetland are immensely popular.

People are drawn to other ancient sites such as stone circles and these have been the focus of many different types of activity. Some people see happenings, like the reborn druids with their midsummer ceremonies at Stonehenge, as central in new forms of pagan worship. Yet others think they may attract UFOs, since suggestions have been made that they are some kind of portal between worlds. The fascination of such sites seems to be growing stronger. The continuing attraction of Arthurian material has been matched over the past few years by a distinctly mystical interest in the thoughts and beliefs of our Celtic ancestors. More books than ever are published on Celtic and even Pictish subjects but we must remember not to lose our critical faculties. The term Celtic, which should apply only to linguistic matters, now surfaces in all sorts of areas and I suppose it is only a matter of time before Arbroath smokies and Forfar bridies are presented as Celtic food!

It has been overlooked by many scholars who have written on 'Celtic' society that the last Celtic-speaking tribal warrior society did not disappear until the eighteenth century in Scotland. When the Highland, Lowland and English followers of Prince Charles Edward Stewart were slaughtered at Culloden on 16 April 1746 it truly was the end o an auld sang. The tribal society of the Gaelic-speaking areas of Scotland was already in terminal decline but it is still a remarkable fact that so little has been written about that society. It is as if the body politic of the British State was put into shock by the Jacobite Rebellion and that Scottish history has been suffering ever since. The classic texts on the Celts concentrate on Irish and Welsh material despite the fact that Celtic society continued for hundreds of years later – here in Scotland. And it was a life in which learning was passed on through story and song.

The history of Scotland has long been obscured because of a few historical events. Little written material survives from ancient times due to various raids and invasions. The earliest of these started in the ninth century with the Vikings, who often raided monasteries – the natural home for written material as well as the precious metals they were seeking. Later came the invasion of the English king Edward Longshanks in the thirteenth century. Edward destroyed all documents he could find as they were sure to undermine his opportunistic and dishonest claims to be sovereign lord of Scotland. What he did not destroy was taken south to England and disappeared.

Later, the Reformation saw the unleashing of fanatical mobs who burned books and destroyed great art, claiming it was all 'Papist'. Because of this and because of the close links between Ireland and Scotland, Scottish culture has come to be presented as an Irish import through Gaelic, or an English import through the medium of Anglo-Saxon, which influenced Scots north of the border.

The heroes that populate our landscape come from various traditions – from the Gaelic Finn MacCool and his Fenian warriors to stories of Arthur and his cheating queen, which have survived from times when people in the Southwest, the East and North spoke an ancestor of modern-day Welsh. There are also tales of giants and giantesses which step straight out of the traditions of

Scandinavia, first told in a language related to the Scots and English we hear today.

Scotland has a complex history indeed and most of it was initially passed on through the spoken word. It is the spoken word attached to the landscape that has provided the material for this book. I have found these stories in earlier published material mainly – often guidebooks and local histories whose authors had no particular interest in legendary material, seeing it only as adding a bit of colour. The nineteenth century in particular saw many such publications, triggered by the start of tourism, given such powerful impetus by the works of Sir Walter Scott. Today as we begin to realise we have had little access to Scotland's actual history, such material takes on new significance.

Recent research in Australia has shown the capability of oral tradition to pass on factual material over thousands of years. Aboriginal tales of giant marsupials, for example, had been dismissed as the fantasy of primitive savages. Excavation of the bones of such creatures, now called diprodotons, and sometimes found in sites over 20,000 years old, tells a different story. Other tales mention vocanic eruptions that have also since been confirmed by excavation. The fact is that while mainstream European scholarship has long asserted that oral tradition was made redundant when writing was introduced, the spoken word has never ceased to be important.

Much of the material in this book has a long pedigree. How long may be impossible to say, but the intriguing possibility is that the story of the raising of the great stone circle of Calanish on Lewis, passed by word of mouth from generation to generation, is true.

Some stories, like those of Finn MacCool or Arthur, exist in many places because they were told in those places and it is part of the traditional art of storytelling to place stories in a landscape the audience knows. Without such location the stories would lose much of their relevance. Such stories include ones of an ancient Mother Goddess known as the *Cailleach* in Gaelic and the Carlin in Scots, stories associated with our magnificent and decidedly moody mountains, tales of lochs and rivers inhabited by supernatural creatures, stories of romance and heroism associated with the

Pictish symbol stones, tales of revenge, and harrowing tales of the persecution of women as witches perhaps because they held on too strongly to the old ways.

We should remember that Scotland has gone through many significant changes since people started arriving here almost 10,000 years ago. Some of these changes we know about, many we never will. What is significant is that the legendary landscape has retained many ancient ideas despite these often substantial changes. The old idea that major change was a result of invasions by increasingly superior and technologically advanced warrior aristocrats is a fantasy of the ruling classes. We now know that the development of new styles of pottery represent technological advance in itself rather than invasion. Language change was also presented as a result of military conquest. The reality is that Scotland has spoken different languages at different times. It has been predominantly P-Celtic-speaking (the ancestor of modern day Welsh) as well as Q-Celtic-speaking (the ancestor of modern day Gaelic) and Germanic-speaking, as today, when most of us have Scots or Scottish-English as our first language. However at different times from the eighth to the eleventh centuries there were Germanic-speaking Norse settlements in different parts of the country and there are suggestions today that Germanic speakers settled here during or after the short visitations of the Romans. There are also suggestions that perhaps Germanic tribes were settling our south-eastern coasts almost as early as the Gaels are said to have founded Dalriada, around 500 AD.

Legendary material, however, has a way of passing by such upheavals – as if the psycho-sociological relevance of the stories runs deeper than language itself within society. This might explain why we have the *Cailleach* in Gaelic matched so precisely by the Carlin in Scots.

Maybe the old ways are not yet totally gone. Apart from resurgences of well-dressing and the Beltane fires, and the survivals of other rituals like the various midwinter fire festivals, these tales can perhaps help us see more clearly how our ancestors lived and what they believed. Industrialisation and literacy are, like the habit of living in cities, very recent in terms of the history of this land,

and our much-loved landscape retains a great deal from earlier times.

I have divided the book into topics which link tales of similar kinds and hope this will lead the reader into a deeper understanding of our landscape and hopefully also into physical exploration of this beautiful, ever-changing and lore-laden land.

CHAPTER 1

The Hollow Hills

IN VARIOUS PARTS OF THE country different heroes are believed to be resting below ground awaiting the call to come forth to the aid of Scotland. It may be that such stories are connected to the ancient beliefs associated with the great chambered cairn burials known throughout our landscape. Scholars nowadays see these as communal burials and no longer as the tombs of kings or other supposed high-status leaders of contemporary society. These chambered tombs often contained the bones of several individuals, though not all of the bones. Skulls and thigh bones seemed to dominate, suggesting a link with the well-known motif on Scottish gravestones, the skull-and-crossbones, portrayed in countless Hollywood films as the flag of pirates. It is now thought that these were the sites of specific rites on the great feast days of the year. Samhain, today conflated with Halloween, was very much a feast of the dead in tribal times. The bones were brought forth at these times and used in rituals in which the spirits of the dead would be asked to ensure that the seeds planted in the earth would grow in the coming spring. This also might help to explain the importance of genealogies or family histories in Scotland, for if you are asking your ancestors for direct help it seems a good idea to be sure of who you are talking to! Such genealogies, passed on by word of mouth, went back for many generations and the *seannachie*, the traditional genealogist of the Highland clans, had his counterpart at the coronation of kings, as well as at the investiture of clan chiefs.

The Eildon Hills

The Eildon Hills (D61) to the south of Melrose in the Borders were known long ago to the invading Romans as Trimontium, the three-peaked hills. It has long been told locally that King Arthur himself is sleeping inside the Eildons awaiting his call to arms.

A local horse-dealer called Canonbie Dick, a fearless character 'wha wid hae sellt a cuddy tae the Deil himsel', was riding home one evening by the Eildons when he was hailed by a man in very old-fashioned dress. He asked to buy the horses Dick had with him and, after some hard bargaining, paid for them in ancient gold coins before disappearing into the night. This happened several times and at last Dick's curiosity got the better of him and he suggested the mysterious stranger take him home for a drink to seal the bargain. Reluctantly, the stranger agreed but warned Dick that he would be going into danger, particularly if he lost his nerve. This only served to intrigue the horse-dealer even more and he urged the stranger to hurry. The stranger led Dick to a hummock on the side of the Eildons still known today as the Lucken Hare, where to Dick's surprise he opened a concealed door in the side of the hill. At once he found himself inside a huge torch-lit cavern full of rows of stalls, and in each stall a sleeping horse waited with a warrior clad in armour. The horses were all black as coal, as was the armour of the sleeping warriors. On a great table lay a massive sword and a horn of like size. The stranger told Dick that he was Thomas of Ercildoun, the famous Thomas the Rhymer, and he uttered the fateful words, 'He that shall sound that horn and draw that sword shall, if his heart fail him not, be king over all broad Britain. But all depends on courage, and much on your taking the sword or horn first.'

Dick took up the horn and with a trembling hand managed to blow a feeble note. In response a thundering sound erupted and the men and horses began to rise. Horses stamped their hooves and snorted as warriors sprang to their feet, sword in hand. Dick was terrified and dropped the horn, reaching his hand to lift the enchanted sword. A great voice rang out:

Woe to the coward that ever he was born
Who did not draw the sword before he blew the horn.

At that a mighty wind came up and Dick was tossed in the air and thrown clean out of the cave. He had made the wrong choice. The following morning he was found lying on the hillside by local shepherds. Lifting his head he told his strange story, fell back and died.

A variant on this story is that once the Rhymer has bought enough coal-black horses the warriors will sally forth from their slumbers to put the world to rights. In other legends the sleeping warriors are King Arthur and his knights awaiting the call to come to the aid of Britain.

It is said that the Eildons are where Thomas Learmont of Ercildoun, now called Earlston (D60), was spirited away by the Queen of the Fairies for seven years. When at last he returned he had the gift of prophecy. Thomas of Ercildoun is believed to have been a real figure who lived in the thirteenth century and many folk rhymes and prophecies are attributed to him. The spot where he was spirited away is marked by a stone where there once was an ancient tree – probably a yew – now known as the Eildon Tree Stone. Such is Thomas the Rhymer's hold on imagination that he is mentioned in several of Scotland's earliest histories and is said to have lived in many parts of the country.

Thomas

There are many versions of his story but all agree he was on Eildon when he saw a fair lady dressed all in green, her horse's mane dressed with silver bells, riding towards him. Taken by both her beauty and her majesty, he doffs his hat and kneels before her. She knows who Thomas is and says that she has come to see him. She takes him up behind her on her horse and she heads for Elfinland. When they come to a red river, Thomas asks what river this can be.

'This,' she tells him, 'is the river of blood that is shed on the earth in one day.'

They ride on and come to a crystal river. Again Thomas asks what river this can be and the Elfin Queen tells him, 'This is the river of tears that is spilled on the earth in one day.'

On and on they ride until they come to a thorny road and Thomas asks what road this can be.

'This is the road you must never set foot on, for this is the road to Hell.'

They ride on and on and come to a great orchard and Thomas asks to be let down so he can have an apple or two for he is hungry and the apples look very fine to him. The Queen tells him he cannot touch them for they are the apples that are made of the curses that fall on the earth in one day. They ride on and she reaches high up into one particular tree and plucks him an apple. She gives him the apple, saying, 'It will give to you a tongue that will never lie.'

And this is how he got the gift of prophecy. They ride further on and at last come to a great and beautiful valley which she tells him is Elfinland. Thomas lived here for seven long years, after which he returned to earth and became a great prophet. It is said that among other things he foretold that the North Sea and the Atlantic Ocean would one day meet through Scotland, and this is taken to mean the Caledonian Canal. Many and varied are the prophecies and rhymes from all over Scotland attributed to Thomas after his return from Elfinland, but a few years later the following is said to have occurred.

A white hind and hart came forth from the forest to Thomas's village. The local people were amazed to see these wondrous creatures in their village and somebody ran to fetch Thomas so he would tell them what this might mean. When Thomas came, he knew at once, bade farewell to his friends and accompanied the deer back into the forest. He was never seen again.

The motif of the deer and particularly the white deer has been associated with pagan religion, and particularly the Mother Goddess, for thousands of years all over Europe. They were fitting messengers from the Elfin Queen to summon Thomas back to Elfinland.

Tomnahurich

Tomnahurich (B16), the hill of the yew trees, is in the centre of Inverness. In the middle of the last century it was chosen as a cemetery – but the yew tree has long been associated with burial grounds, possibly because it lives so long that it seemed eternal to our ancestors. Some yew trees, like the famous one at Fortingall (D29) in Perthshire, live for thousands of years. The Fortingall yew tree may be the oldest living organism in Europe.

There is a story concerning Tomnahurich which has changed its clothes many times over the years.

Not long ago two sturdy but wild-looking, young, kilted lads were seen in the centre of Inverness. Both were carrying bag-pipes and shouting at all the passing cars – in Gaelic. It was just a matter of time before the police were called and the two young lads locked up in the local jail. In the morning they appeared before the sheriff, who fortunately had the Gaelic himself. They told him their story.

One night, they told him, they were on their way to Inverness from Strathspey to play in the streets when they were stopped on the road by an old man. He offered them a guinea apiece and as much whisky as they could drink if they would pipe for him and a few of his friends. This was a very good offer and they accepted at once.

The old man led them up the side of Tomnahurich. Halfway up the ancient, sacred mound they came across a great wooden door which the old man opened. They stepped inside to a great ballroom full of beautifully dressed, handsome men and women, all waiting to dance. They were given a dram, then another, and then they were ordered to play. As they did, the place came alive and all through the night the pipers played – refreshed with regular drams of the very finest whisky.

At last the dance came to an end and the old man thanked them, gave them a guinea each and led them to the door. It was then that they started to get worried: the city had changed suddenly and there were strange, hard, noisy beasts in the streets. They told the sheriff they had concealed their golden guineas from the police thus far, but now they handed them over to him only to watch the coins crumble into dust.

They were returned to the cells and a minister was called to have a word with them. One of them then told the clergyman that he had been at the Battle of Sherrifmuir (D35) the week before. The Battle of Sherrifmuir took place in the seventeenth century! At once the minister began to intone a prayer. As soon as the name of God was mentioned, the pipers, their pipes and clothes crumbled into a pile of dust around the minister's feet.

This story is told in many places in Scotland, sometimes with fiddlers instead of pipers, and it seems to combine a belief in the fairies with an ongoing respect for places of ancient sanctity, as well as providing a very good tale for a winter's night. Tomnahurich, though, was believed to be the main meeting place for the fairies in all of the Highlands which led to its alternative name, *Tom na Sìtheachan*, the hill of the fairies. In some versions one of the musicians is smart enough to stick a knife or other iron object in the door of the fairy hill, thus ensuring his escape. (This because the fairies are said to come from a time before iron and therefore the metal acts as a countercharm to their wiles.)

Calton Hill

Another famous fairy hill is Calton Hill overlooking Princes Street in the heart of Edinburgh (D56, 57).

Around the year 1660 a seaman called Captain Burton was witness to a remarkable event. He had been told of a young lad called the Fairy Boy who had the second sight. Burton was intrigued and arranged to meet the boy. The lad told the captain that every Thursday night he would take his drum to Calton Hill. There, a great pair of gates in the side of the hill would open. He would enter and play for the fairies as they danced through the night. There was a great deal of feasting and drinking and on occasion they would all fly off through the air to France or Holland and hold their revelry there. The Captain was sceptical, but the boy said he was bound to attend these celebrations every Thursday and that all of Scotland could not keep him away. Intrigued, Burton assembled a group of his friends the next Thursday and they met the Fairy Boy in a hostelry. They intended to keep him in conversation until past his supposed appointed hour at which point they thought they would force him to confess to making it all up. But an hour before midnight they suddenly realised that he had managed to slip away from them. They rushed out into the night and headed towards the hill. They found the lad and dragged him back to the tavern, but within minutes he had gone again and this time could not be found. It was thought he had managed to go and join his fairy friends.

Today, Calton Hill is also the site of Beltane rites and probably was at other significant times of the year in earlier centuries. Its name means 'hill of the hazels'. Hazel trees provided the nuts used in divination, particularly at Halloween, and in ancient belief in the Celtic-speaking world the hazel was a sacred tree, particularly its nuts.

The Fairy Boy

The Beltane festival on Calton Hill was accompanied by the Robin Hood Games – a day when all kinds of mischief took place, a celebration frowned on after the Reformation.

You can get a clear idea of what was going on from some of the characters involved in the games. One of the principal characters was the Abbot of Misrule and in the games Robin Hood and Little John were seen as representatives of the common people and would fight with bishops and noblemen. There was a considerable amount of drinking and general mayhem.

In the eighteenth century great religious gatherings with several preachers seem to have taken on some of the aspects of these more ancient assemblies, as can be seen from Robert Burns's poem 'The Holy Fair'. After the Reformation the Kirk decided to suppress the games themselves, but it took several years, fines and even imprisonment before the people gave up this ancient practice.

The revival of Beltane on such a site has a certain sense to it and its attraction can be seen in the ever-increasing number of young people and families who attend.

The Fairy Hill of Aberfoyle

Aberfoyle (C11), in the heart of the magnificent Trossachs, has its own fairy hill which is the focus of a remarkable story.

In 1679 the local minister, Robert Kirk, published *The Secret Commonwealth of Elves, Fauns and Fairies*, an investigation into ancient beliefs among the Highland population. In this book he stated that many Highlanders believed that their ancestors' spirits lived in the fairy hills – a possibility remarkably close to what seems to have been the belief of the people who raised the chambered cairns thousands of years before – and that for every churchyard there would be a fairy mound where the souls of the dead might pass. There the souls would remain until the Day of Judgement. It was a matter of faith that no one should ever interfere with such mounds as this would displease the 'little people' and bring misfortune to anyone who disturbed them.

This amalgam of beliefs finds a strange echo in the fate of Reverend Kirk himself. Kirk was a seventh son and had been born with the gift of second sight – a talent which is seen as a curse as often as a blessing. All in all, the tone of *The Secret Commonwealth* and its great detail make it easy to believe that Kirk had a belief in 'the people of peace'. *The Secret Commonwealth* contains very detailed descriptions of the fairies and how they behaved, and local people believed that he had gone too far: the fairies were extremely displeased to have their secrets disclosed.

One day while he was walking on the fairy hill of Aberfoyle he fell down dead and local people said it was the work of the fairies. After his funeral his spirit came to a relative and told him that he was not dead but that he had been taken away to Fairyland. He asked him to pass on a message to another cousin, Graham of Duchray. The message was that at the forthcoming baptism of his son he would appear in the room. At that point Duchray was to throw the knife or dirk he held in his hand over the spirit's head and the spell would be broken and Kirk would return, alive. But, he said, 'If this be neglected, I am lost forever.'

The appointed day came and, true to his word, Kirk appeared.

His cousin Duchray was so astonished that he could not bring himself to throw the knife. The spirit of the lost minister disappeared and has never been seen since.

The Two Hunchbacks

Near Kilchrenan (C23) by Loch Awe there is a fairy mound with an interesting tale. The story is known all over the world and I first heard it as a joke in a Dundee pub, which just illustrates how tenacious the ideas of our ancestors can be!

In a clachan near Kilchrenan there lived two hunchbacks, Hamish and Handy who, although going to the same school, having the same age and suffering from the same deformity, were like chalk and cheese. Hamish was a capable, kindly lad while Handy was an idle, worthless chiel with a wicked tongue. He took great delight in making Hamish miserable any chance he got.

Hamish was deeply in love with a lass called Morag, a local beauty, and when one day he realised this, Handy told everyone that such a beauty would have nothing to do with a deformed creature like Hamish. After finishing work that same day Hamish wandered off on his own and sat down on a hillside where he burst into tears. Suddenly he heard his name being spoken and

The two hunchbacks

looked up to see a small but beautiful woman dressed all in green. She asked what was wrong and he poured out his heart to her, telling her all about his feelings for Morag and his problems with Handy. The woman smiled and told him to come that night to a wee green knoll, to knock on the hill and say '*Fosgail an dorus*' three times – 'Open the door'.

That night Hamish made his way to the knoll and, knocking gently on the hill with the stick he needed to help him walk, he said the magic words. At once a door opened and he stepped inside. He found himself in a large well-lit chamber full of the wee folk, with beautiful music filling the air. Seated on a dais in the centre of it all was the woman he had met earlier whom he now realised was the Queen of the Fairies herself. She explained that she had taken pity on him and asked if he would like her to cast a spell on Morag to make her love him. Hamish said no, he did not think it fair to have Morag fall for a wee twisted creature like himself.

'What would you have?' asked the queen.

'Make me like other men,' said Hamish, 'straight and tall.'

Hardly were the words out of his mouth when he found himself looking down at the little people: his hunchback had disappeared! The queen smiled and asked what he thought of his chances with Morag now. Hamish could hardly speak in his excitement and stammered that he would have to wait and see.

The very next moment he was outside the fairy hill and rushing home. His new appearance gave him new confidence and he went to Morag and told her how he felt. She saw before her a well-built handsome young man with a kindly air and a sparkle in his eyes and soon he was ahead of all her other suitors in her affections.

Handy was beside himself with jealousy when he saw what had happened and he came to Hamish demanding how he had managed to change himself. Despite Handy's past actions Hamish was never a lad to hold a grudge and freely told Handy what had happened, stressing that he must say the appropriate phrase only three times, no more no less. Handy immediately started planning for what he could do once he too had got rid of his hunchback.

That night, bursting with excitement, Handy approached the knoll. He stamped heavily on the wee hill, shouting out '*Fosgail an dorus*' three times, then a few times more for good measure. In all he shouted it seven times.

Right enough the door opened and he was pulled in. But it was no scene of merriment and pleasure he found. The fairies were indignant and stood around him ominously. Handy looked at the queen but made no gesture of respect. He was asked what he wanted and he told them he wanted what Hamish had been given. At that point one of the fairies tweaked his coat and the head-strong Handy skelped him across the ear. Immediately he found himself birling through the air. The next thing, he was alone on the wee hillock with Hamish's hump on his back as well as his own.

When the story came out he was greatly pitied but many people could not help but laugh, and soon he was left to wander who knows where.

In time Morag agreed to be Hamish's wife and when they were married and raising a family they never passed the fairy hill of Kilchrenan without a good word or kind thought for the little people.

CHAPTER 2

The Goddess in the Landscape

ALL PAGAN RELIGIONS IN Europe have come through a 'goddess phase' and there is no reason to think Scotland should have been any different. Behind tales of witches, supernatural females and female saints lies a reality that is still manifest in our landscape – a goddess walked these lands, and perhaps still does. In ancient religions life was seen to emanate from a female source and the landscape of Scotland is dotted with references to the female principle in its nurturing, life-giving sense, though we also have dark, violent females suggesting the destructive aspect of a goddess, in short life and death.

Many of the most striking of our hills are called paps, and in Gaelic *cioch* and *mam* both refer to the differing shapes of the female breast. We have the Paps of Jura (C19), the Paps of Fife, the Pap of Glencoe (A23), the Maiden Paps (D65) in Roxburghshire, Maiden Pap (B6) in Sutherland and many others. There is also Bennachie (B44) (originally *Beinn na Cioch*) and Lochnagar (B42), initially *Beinn na Ciochan*, with its own *Caisteal na Caillich*, Meikle Pap and Little Pap. There are many others, but the fact that they have been named after the shape of the female breast is perhaps not enough to conclude that we are seeing remnants of a goddess and her cult. However, when we find holy wells and symbolic placenames associated with ritual and mythology and early sacred sites around such places it seems possible that goddess worship was involved in the naming of such physical features.

The Cailleach

In many parts of Scotland that were once Gaelic-speaking – which is most of the country – there are tales of the *Cailleach*, a name meaning 'old woman' or 'hag'. In many of the old tales however she is presented as the Spirit of Winter, keeping Bride, the Goddess of Summer imprisoned until she is released by her lover. As we shall see, the Cailleach in Gaelic tradition is matched by the figure of the Carlin in Scots tradition. There are literally dozens of placenames referring to the Cailleach and many such tales are attached to mountains.

The Cailleach

One of the oldest tales of this kind refers to Scotland's greatest natural wonder. This is the Corryvreckan (C17), a great whirlpool between the Inner Hebridean islands of Jura (C18) and Scarba. Just off Scarba's south coast there is a huge underwater spike and when the Atlantic waters are forced through the Sound of Jura and meet tidal surges coming around both islands the waters start to gyrate around this spike and the whirlpool Corryvreckan is formed. It is at its most violent at the end of autumn although sailors who dare to cross it are always in danger at any time of the year.

The name of the Corryvreckan comes from *Coire Bhreacain*, the cauldron of the plaid. The cauldron is associated with goddesses throughout Celtic and Germanic mythology and legend, which may be why it is represented so widely on Pictish symbol stones, but here it has a specific meaning. It was in this great cauldron that the Cailleach washed her plaid, the traditional one-piece garment of the Highlands. It was this washing that was said to have created the whirlpool in autumn, the sound of which can be heard for many miles around. After washing her plaid the Cailleach is said to lay her plaid over the hills of west Scotland to dry. As she is the oldest being, her plaid is pure white – it needed no colour to differentiate her from other beings. This is, of course, a mythological explanation for the first snows of the year, linked to the greatest physical event in the landscape of Scotland and her surrounding waters. Some scholars link the Cailleach to Ben Nevis specifically. Like many of our hills it has an *Allt na Cailleach*, stream of the Cailleach.

This is essentially the same Cailleach located in different parts of Scotland, as in *Caillich na Mointich*, the Cailleach of the moors, whose form lies in the hills to the south of the great stone circle of Calanish, which we shall look at later.

Time and again we find the Cailleach associated with mountains, and on a clear day as the weather changes it is easy to see why. I recall standing on a hillside in Glen Clova looking north to Lochnagar in early autumn on a bright day with a few clouds high in the sky. As I watched, clouds began to form around the head of Lochnagar and as the sky darkened clouds began to stream out from the mountain. A goddess, of course, creates the weather as well as the planet and all its beings and it seems only natural that she should be located on our mountain tops. The harsh black figures of the Cailleach associated with Bein Bhreac in Lochaber, Ben Wyvis (B10) in Easter Ross and many other Scottish mountains seem particularly apt creatures to be associated with Scottish winters which every year exact a toll of sacrifice from among the walkers and climbers who venture amongst them.

One of the strongest associations of the Cailleach is with the deer. Jura, mentioned above, means 'deer isle'. The Cailleach there, *Cailleach Mhor nam Fiadh*, big cailleach of the deer, is said to have no remorse in killing any non-Jura man who sets foot on her island. This is very close to the notion of a goddess representing the land, and connects to the Celtic idea of a new king marrying the female representation of the land and thereby attaining sovereignty. Many *cailleachs* are mentioned as helping deer hunters who approach them the right way.

Ben Cruachan (C24), which soars over the north side of the road between Dalmally and Oban, has its own Cailleach story. Here the Cailleach was the guardian of a well on the summit of the mountain. Every evening she had to cover the well with a large flat stone and every morning take it off again. One night she was tired out after being out all day with her herds in Connel and fell asleep by the side of the well. Night fell and still she slept. Up came the waters of the well and flooded out over the land, rushing down the side of the mountain to the south. As the flood began to rage it broke through the Pass of Brander with a great roar and the Cailleach sprang awake. Try as she might she could not cap the well and the torrent flowed free, drowning many a man and beast caught in its path. This is how Loch Awe was formed and it is said the Cailleach was so ashamed that she turned to stone and the stone still sits among the rocky ruins overlooking the Loch.

Here, as with the Corryvreckan, we have the Cailleach being instrumental in the formation of the landscape. The same story of the overflowing well has given us the origin of Loch Ness and other lochs. It is no surprise that tradition also tells us that the Cailleach formed the Western Isles when an apronful of stones she was carrying for the making of Scotland accidentally fell!

On Mull the Carn na Caillich (A21) is where the Cailleach dropped a load of stones when the strap of the creel she was carrying the stones in broke. She is said to have been trying to build a bridge over the Sound of Mull and intended to put chains across the Sound of Islay to stop ships passing.

The stone circle of Calanais laid out on the ground in the shape of a Celtic cross over five thousand years ago is truly one of Scotland's wonders. Its use in lunar observation is now accepted and in the hills along which the moon 'dances' at the end of its 18.6 year cycle we can see how important the notion of a goddess in the landscape must have been. In these hills to the south of the Calanais complex the outline of a reclining human figure can be seen. Though it is only recently that archaeologists have rediscovered the lunar associations of this magnificent megalithic site, local tradition has preserved at least one memory of the sanctity of the area. The term for the human figure reclining in the hills to the south is *Cailleach na Mointich* – Cailleach of the moors. In this case, the Cailleach may be a goddess, here present to underline the importance of the complex of megalithic sites around Loch Roag.

In a tale told all over the Highlands, the Cailleach – in this case, a great, black-faced hag – has Bride, the Goddess of Summer, imprisoned. In some versions they are mother and daughter. During the winter while Bride is imprisoned, the Cailleach goes around the country hammering the land with her great hammer and thus freezing it. Bride is given the impossible task of washing a brown fleece white while the Cailleach is out and about. Far off in the Land of Eternal Youth, Angus Og dreams of the beautiful maiden harshly imprisoned and resolves to come to her rescue.

Bride herself manages to escape on the 1st of February for three days but is soon recaptured. This is supposed to account for the three days of good weather that were said to happen at the beginning of February.

Meanwhile Angus Og searches everywhere for Bride, and with the help of a mysterious male figure eventually locates her. He frees her and the couple are initially pursued by the Cailleach. But with Bride's release spring has come and the Cailleach's powers fade quickly. At last she gives up the chase in disgust and throws her hammer under a holly bush – which is why nothing ever grows there. Bride and Angus Og are married and rule together over the summer months until once again the Cailleach's time comes round.

This tale comes from long before the calendars were changed at the end of the sixteenth century so it is perhaps surprising how a short spell of good weather does indeed occur at the beginning of February sometimes. Or did the new calendar simply put things back in balance?

The Carlin

In the east of Scotland, Scots-speaking for almost as long as Gaelic has been spoken in the west, there is a figure who is a clear match for the Cailleach. This is the Carlin who, like her counterpart, has left traces in the landscape.

On the western side of the Lomond Hills, of which the Paps of Fife form part, is the narrow gap known as Glenvale. Here stood a striking pillar of stone known as Carlin Maggie, which sadly has now fallen. The tale is that this was a witches' haunt and Carlin Maggie was their leader. One time seeing Satan approach carrying a load of rocks she took a stand on Bishop's Hill (D40) and proceeded to flyte him – insult him in rhyme. He dropped his load of rocks and chased her, coming close enough to turn her into stone at a spot overlooking Loch Leven. Here we have a representative of the old, pagan religion going against even the Christian Devil! In the surrounding area there are records of fertility rituals associated with a nearby hole called the Maiden Bore (D41), old wells and even an early Christian 'fish' sign carved in the living rock on

West Lomond Hill. The clustering of such sites strongly supports the idea that such names were given in honour of a goddess and that the area was one of considerable sanctity.

The Carlin was the subject of one early anonymous poem, 'The Gyre-Carling', in which she is said to have farted out North Berwick Law! The poem was said to have been a favourite of James V. This is a bit different from the other tales here but still links her directly to the creation of the physical world and it is interesting that one of our most famous groups of witches gathered in the shade of North Berwick Law (D54). The name Gyre-Carling means something like the biting or ravenous old woman, very like the meaning of the *Cailleach Bheur*, a name that crops up often in Gaelic tradition.

The Gyre-Carling in the poem is also remarkably like the Cailleach in the poem 'The Manere of the Crying of Ane Playe' by William Dunbar, the great fifteenth/sixteenth century poet. There, as the wife of Finn,

She spittit Lochlomond with her lips;
Thunner and fireflaucht flew fae her hips.

'Fireflaucht' is lightning and this may be a reference to her role as the source of storms and bad weather. The similarity between the Cailleach and Carlin here is absolute.

A striking suggestion of ancient worship and ritual comes from Loch Carlingwark (C2) in Dumfries and Galloway. Here in the loch a great collection of votive gifts was found – gifts put into wells, rivers or lochs accompanying prayers to a goddess, or perhaps a god. Among the collection from Carlingwark, to be seen in the Museum of Scotland, is a great cauldron, echoing the relationship between many early goddess figures and the actual source of food for family and communities. Water has also long been central to pagan religion and accounts for the long association of prayer and ritual with wells, as we shall see later.

Bride / St Brigit

One tale that occurs in several locations tells how on the morning of Beltane, the Cailleach went to a holy well. Taking a mouthful of water just as the sun rose, she drank and was magically transformed into the summer goddess, Bride, the possible forerunner of St Brigit who has long been revered in Ireland and Scotland. This story corresponds to the old notion of the year being split into two main seasons – the 'time of the Big Sun' and the 'time of the Little Sun'. These seasons were separated by the great feasts of Beltane and Samhain. Although the other great quarter-day feasts of Imbolc (1 February) and Lammas (1 August) were undoubtedly important they are clearly overshadowed by the other two. Imbolc itself is 'Bride's day' and was linked to the start of lambing.

St Brigit is essentially the Christianised version of an earlier goddess whose popularity in Ireland spread to Scotland. She may have been mother goddess of the Brigantes, a British tribe from present-day northwestern England. She is closely matched in Norse mythology by Freyja.

Brigit survives in Gaelic tradition as the birthmaid of Christ. As we shall see later, there are many Bride's Wells in Scotland and the number of Kilbrides shows the extent of churches once dedicated to her. However, there are other Brigit names that suggest a strong connection to the earlier goddess figure.

In Glen Clova in the Angus foothills of the Grampians there is a pool by the roadside just east of the Gella bridge called Bride's Coggie (a coggie is Old Scots for a wooden bucket). In the same area there are placenames which refer to women which might give more weight to the idea of a goddess site here. There is Clachnabrain which comes from the Gaelic *Clach na Mnathan*, the stone of the women, and Braeminzeon which is *Braigh na Mnathan*, hillside of the women. Near Bride's Coggie in the shadow of the Craigs of Lethnot was the first location of a church in the glen. In a story that is repeated throughout the country we are told that the stones of the church were always moved overnight from the selected spot until the site itself was changed. In a glen just a few kilometres to the east, Glenesk (D3), is Bride's Bed, which may refer to an ancient man-made circular depression below Craigmaskeldie (D2) at the head of the glen. Also in Angus is Bride's Ring (D17), the remains of a prehistoric defensive structure.

Several examples of the rituals associated with Bride and St Brigit have been described in the past. In the Western Isles where Bride's importance is emphasised in her title as 'handmaiden to Mary' or 'birthmaid to Christ', intricate procedures accompanied Imbolc. Old women would make an oblong basket in the shape of a cradle, which they would call *leabaidh Bride*, Bride's bed. They would then take pains to decorate it with primroses, daisies and other flowers that open their eyes in the morning of the year. These would have been gathered from sunny sheltered valleys nearby. After that they would take a sheaf of corn and fashion it into the shape of a woman which they would then dress up with brightly-coloured ribbons, sparkling sea shells and bright stones from the hill. When it was all dressed and decorated, one of the women would go to the door of the house and, standing on the step with her hands on the jambs, call quietly into the darkness, 'Bride's bed is ready.' Another woman behind her would reply, 'Let Bride come in. Bride is welcome.' Then the woman at the door would again address Bride: 'Bride, come thou in, thy bed is made. Preserve the house for the Trinity.'

With great ceremony the women would lay the figure of Bride in the bed. A small straight white wand (the bark having been peeled off) would then be placed beside the figure. These wands were generally of birch, broom, bramble, white willow or other sacred wood. The women would then level the ashes on the hearth, smoothing them over carefully. The following morning the whole family would make a close examination of the ashes. If they found the mark of the wand of Bride they would rejoice, but if what they found was *lorg Bride*, the footprint of Bride, they

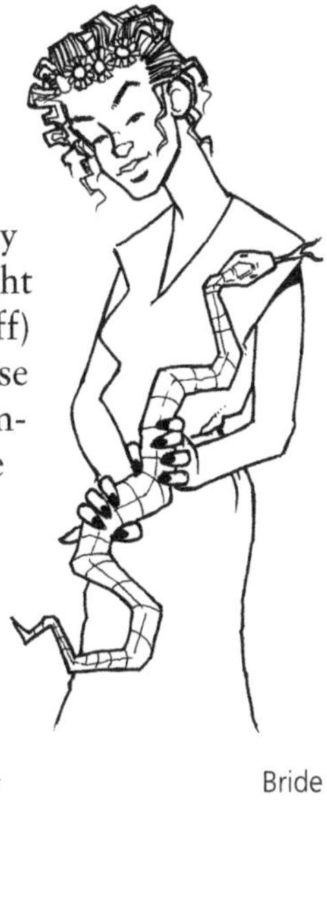

Bride

would have cause for great celebration, for this was taken to mean that Bride herself was present in their home during the night. This was widely believed to mean that there would be increase in family, in flock and in field in the coming year. If there were no marks on the ashes, the family would be disappointed, for they thought that this was a sign that Bride was offended and had not heard their call. They would then make offerings to try and propitiate her. This is clearly nothing to do with Christianity, even if Bride was 'the birthmaid of Christ'.

Within Gaelic tradition there is one association with Bride that stands out as a particularly strong echo of pre-Christian thought and that is her association with the serpent. The serpent in Christian terms is of course evil, but several rhymes survive showing that Bride was directly associated with this unlikely creature. In Scottish terms the association is specifically with the adder, our only indigenous snake. It is also of course a creature strongly linked with various traditions regarding those most romantic and insubstantial figures, the druids. McNeill in *The Silver Bough* gives this version of a hymn to the adder which was believed to emerge from its hibernation on Imbolc (St Brigit's Day, or 1 February):

> Today is the day of Bride.
> The serpent shall come from the hole.
> I will not molest the serpent
> Nor will the serpent molest me.

This has been commented upon as a relic of serpent worship by several commentators but it is probably truer to say that the serpent/adder is a symbol associated with a Mother Goddess. The serpent has been seen by many cultures as a symbol of knowledge. The creature's habits of shedding its skin and of hibernating underground make it a good symbol for the ideas of regeneration and rebirth. In ancient times when prayers were said to try and ensure the harvest for the coming season, the serpent's association with the earth itself was also significant. There are scholars who think that our ancestors prayed to those who had gone before them to work magic on the seeds in the earth to ensure harvest the following year. The appearance of a variety of serpent/adder representations on Pictish symbol stones strongly suggests they saw it as a powerful religious symbol and it is not impossible that they associated it with Bride herself.

We should remember that these practices are recorded as happening in communities that had been ostensibly Christian for over a thousand years! The idea of Bride, an aspect of a Mother Goddess, continued to have a hold on both community and individual until very recently. Just as Bride is associated with the serpent, the Cailleach is associated with the cauldron (another symbol found on the Pictish symbol stones). As the passage above illustrates, there were also rituals associated with such figures – rituals that might come from as far back as the Stone Age.

CHAPTER 3

The Cateran

MANY WRITERS HAVE TOLD OF the bleak harshness of Rannoch Moor (C25), the windswept, boggy area of Scotland between Loch Rannoch and Glencoe. This is an area where the weather is harsh for much of the year, where there is little shelter and seemingly little life. Yet this apparently barren area is the site of stories that have been passed down by word of mouth, giving us a picture of a period of our history that has yet to be clearly understood.

For this is the area in the years after Culloden where the Cateran gathered. Cateran is a Gaelic word originally meaning warrior, but due to the habits and practices of ancient tribal warrior society in Scotland it has become linked to one activity specifically: cattle-raiding. From Iron Age times the warrior tribes of Britain counted their wealth in cattle, and even into the eighteenth century this ancient way of life survived, warriors proving themselves by lifting another clan's cattle. This was not considered theft; it was how the warriors showed their skill and courage and was particularly important for anyone who hoped to lead the clan. For we must remember that if a chief was not up to his job, clan society had ways and means of making sure someone else took his place. It is also true to say that the hereditary chief was not always the leader in battle. Rather, this was likely to be the role of the best or most skilful of the warriors of the clan, and owed as much to intelligence and creativity as to strength of arm.

Serjeant Mor

The highland warriors who gathered in the autumn on Rannoch in the years after 1746 were the last remnants of a dying society. The smashing of the Jacobite army on Culloden Moor on 16 April that year was followed by widespread killings and repression throughout the Highland area. As often as not, other Scots were responsible for the slaughter and rapine, but they were without doubt following a government policy designed to eradicate independent clans for ever. The survivors of Culloden who gathered in Rannoch no doubt knew their days were numbered, but facing execution or exile, they had made their decision. By this period the traditional cattle-raiding had broken down and for a while many clans raided the more prosperous lowlands. Now they felt justified in taking cattle, and even the personal possessions of anyone who had supported the Hanoverian cause. Presbyterian ministers were a prime target in the late 1740s. The raids on the Lowlands over the previous half century and longer had led to a curious situation where some clansmen acted as guardians of cattle against other clans. It is one of the ironies of Scottish history that contracts of blackmail from these times have survived, revealing blackmail was as much a form of insurance as of extortion.

The men in Rannoch would raid anywhere they could. In response, the government had four- to twelve-man garrisons in every glen in Angus, Aberdeenshire, Inverness-shire, Perthshire, much of Sutherland and parts of Argyll. These garrisons were linked by mounted patrols but the Cateran were active until 1753

Sergeant Mor

when the most famous of them, Serjeant Mor, was hanged at Perth (82). In this period not only were the Highlanders banned from carrying their traditional weaponry of dirk, sword and pistols or musket, but the wearing of a kilt and the playing of bagpipes were also banned – except in those British army regiments which were formed from the 'loyal' clans.

Iain Dubh Cameron had served in the French army and when Prince Charles Edward Stewart raised the Jacobite Rebellion he resigned his post and came back to Scotland. A veritable giant of a man, the Serjeant Mor became the subject of many tales in the years after Culloden when the Cateran were hidden and made up by the Highland population – despite the presence and repressive activities of the British army. Surviving stories and situation reports from the garrisons themselves describe what we would nowadays call a guerrilla war. Not only was Serjeant Mor adept in the traditional art of cattle-lifting, he was a shining example of the Highland idea of honour.

One day somewhere in or near the Mamore range south of Ben Nevis, Serjeant Mor came across a mounted Englishman with a heavily laden pack horse. He addressed the man, politely noting that there was something of the military man about him though he was not wearing the red coat of the British army. Although initially alarmed at the sight of this big, traditionally dressed Highlander, the Englishman soon began to relax. He said he was heading for Fort William (A24), had lost his way and asked if he could be pointed towards the right road. Serjeant Mor offered to take him on his way. Delighted, the Englishman revealed that he had been very worried that he might be apprehended by the dreadful Serjeant Mor since he was the paymaster carrying all the soldiers' wages. The Highlandman rode alongside saying nothing as the man went on and on about monstrous Serjeant Mor, and the depredations he had been carrying out against man and beast throughout the Highlands. At last they came in sight of the road to Fort William.

At this the giant Highlander spoke. 'There is your way clear before you. As to what you say of the Serjeant Mor, it is all untrue. He is a soldier, not a thief. And apart from one sad occasion in

Strathspey, no-one but a soldier has ever died at the hands of him or his men.'

'How do you know this?' asked the Englishman.

'My name is Iain Dubh Cameron; I am the Serjeant Mor,' came the reply, 'There before you is the road to Inverlochy Castle; you cannot mistake it. You and your money are safe. Tell your governor in future to be sending a more wary messenger with his gold. You can tell him that although I am forced to live as an outlaw I am as much a soldier as he is and I would despise lifting his gold from a defenceless man who confided in me.'

At that the Highlander turned his horse and headed back into the hills leaving a flustered, dumbfounded but heartily relieved paymaster to gallop into Fort William.

After seven years of dodging the troops and supplying a butcher in Perth with a constant supply of fresh meat (to mutual advantage), Serjeant Mor was at last caught at Dunan, just to the east of Rannoch Moor. Already several of his companions had been caught and hanged, but his own capture had required treachery: he had been sold out by one he considered a friend. That so-called friend was made to quit Scotland soon after by the force of local opinion.

To the last Serjeant Mor kept his dignity, never changing his position that he was a soldier in the army of the legitimate heir to the throne. When he was eventually tried and found guilty in Perth, the court still had the ancient office of doomster. His role was to come to court once a sentence of death was passed and place his hand on the head of the prisoner to intimate that his fate was now sealed. As Cameron was sentenced to death by hanging the judge rang a small bell and the black-clad doomster entered and approached the prisoner. Despite being heavily chained, Serjeant Mor struggled to his feet and straining mightily, freed an arm.

'Keep that caitiff [fool] off me. Let him not be touching me or I will give him a terrible skelp,' roared the irate giant.

The doomster fled the court in terror but nothing could prevent the sentence being carried out. On 23 November 1753 Serjeant Mor was hanged at the Burgh Muir in Perth. After this the Highlands were quiet.

Cam Ruadh

On the A93, the road from Blairgowrie to Braemar, there is a dangerous turn overhanging a sheer drop, generally known as the Devil's Elbow. Overlooking the road to the west is the mountain Cairnwell (D9), which gave its name to the pass. The old stagecoach to Braemar used to stop here at a spot known as Kateran's Howe. Passengers would have seen fourteen mounds in the howe, or hollow. These were the graves of raiders from Argyll killed in the mid-seventeenth century Battle of Cairnwell, the largest of which was over two metres long, said to be that of a chieftain of the MacDairmaid sept of Clan Campbell. This was John Grant, known as *Cam Ruadh*, which translates as something like Twisted Redhead. For generations after his death his birthplace was said to be either Glen Taitnach off Glenshee (D5) or Alltnahait in Glen Clunie (B41). This rivalry led to many disputes and some blood being spilt by inhabitants of both places.

Cam Ruadh was well-named. He was little more than five feet tall, stockily built with bow legs and flat feet. His broad flat face had a pug nose and beady eyes, his cheeks were red and blotchy with protuberant veins. Below each eye his cheekbones jutted out crudely and his face was covered in thin straggly red bristles. His one good eye was of a brilliant blue but the other was an opaque horror, streaked with red and permanently open. His lips were thin, barely covering his uneven, squint teeth. All of this was topped off by an unruly thatch of coarse red hair said to resemble nothing so much as a hedgehog.

His voice was thin and squeaky, and he was stubborn, quick-tempered and possessed of a truly waspish tongue. He was as cunning as a fox and as tenacious as a bulldog. Despite this, he had married young and it seems was a good husband. He was also phenomenally strong, without match as a runner in both speed and stamina, and though an excellent swordsman his greatest skill was with the bow. It is told of him that with his one good eye he could see a bluebottle on grey stone at twenty yards and hit it with one shot. No one in living memory had ever shot an arrow more than half as far as Cam Ruadh and it was said he could hit a

Cam Ruadh

midgie or fell an ox with a single arrow. With these skills he was a valued member of his clan and often involved in the fights and skirmishes that sometimes accompanied cattle-raiding.

When pursuers caught up with raiders, sometimes the matter was settled by means of single combat, sometimes by battle between pre-selected numbers and occasionally by wholesale fighting. The Battle of Cairnwell, triggered by the Argyll men lifting cattle from Glen Isla and Glenshee, was one of the latter.

As usual the cattle had been lifted during the night and when the theft was discovered in the morning the men from Isla and Glenshee gathered to give chase, sending a messenger off to Braemar for further help as it seemed the cleansers, as raiders were often called, were numerous. But then a dispute broke out about who had the right to lead the chase and the Glenshee men set off by themselves, followed by the Glen Isla men at a distance. Cam Ruadh stood back from all discussion: he had taken an oath the day before not to draw a bowstring for twenty-four hours, for it is said that he was growing sick of killing.

The Glenshee men ran off after the reivers and came up with them in the Pass of Cairnwell. Leading them was the Glenshee smith and his seven stalwart sons. They pressed ahead and attacked the Argyll men on their own as the Glen Isla men looked on from a nearby ridge. Heavily outnumbered they fell one by one and as each one fell the smith cried, 'Fight today, lads. Grieve tomorrow,' until at last he was cut down. He looked around in vain for the men from Braemar as one of the Argyll men came forward to finish him off. It was noon and the sun shone straight above him. The reiver lifted his sword to send the smith to join his sons and there was a twanging sound followed by a dull thud as the Argyll man was transfixed by an arrow. The smith breathed his last, smiling.

Cam Ruadh had watched in grief as his friends died but with the coming of noon his vow was over and he could join the fray. He had crept quietly behind a stone overlooking the Argyll men as arrow after arrow fell among them, each one finding its mark.

The men from Cromar were in turmoil – where was the mysterious bowman? The rain of death continued until a dozen men lay dead or dying including their mighty chieftain. Then a gust of wind lifted a corner of Cam Ruadh's plaid and the cleansers charged towards him. His bowstring snapped and Cam Ruadh cursed, throwing his bow at the approaching warriors. He turned and ran uphill. Several of his pursuers fired at him but with their friends in their line of fire they soon stopped.

The distance between them grew and, try as they might to speed up, the man before them drew away. One of the leading Argyll men knelt and took aim. The arrow fled true and thudded into John Grant's back. A cheer went up among the Cromar men but it choked back as they saw him continue running up-hill as if nothing had happened. Within seconds he was out of bowshot. Another cheer rang out from the Glenshee men still battling in the pass.

It was answered by another from Meall Ordhar. The Braemar men had arrived! At this the onlookers from Glen Isla joined in and began to charge towards the men from Argyll. Realising they were seriously outnumbered they turned and fled, leaving the lifted cattle they had fought so hard to defend behind them.

It was a great victory but one fought at a terrible price. The Braemar men were hard put to prevent the Glenshee men from spilling the blood of the contingent from Glen Isla. Cam Ruadh silently took all the congratulations but refused all help, the shaft still sticking out from his shoulder. A few hours later they came home and as they passed through the glen several women shouted to Cam Ruadh that he had an arrow in his back, to which he replied every time, 'I know that myself already.'

On reaching his own croft the wee man sat on a stool and told his wife to pull the arrow from his back. She tugged and tugged, with never a sound from her man. But the arrow would not budge so he lay flat on his face and his wife stood on his back, a foot on either side of the shaft. At his word she bent and pulled with all her might. Out came the arrow with a lump of her husband's flesh. His wife then bound up the wound and Cam Ruadh proceeded to have a vast meal of venison, which all the Highlanders believed could do them nothing but good.

The Battle of Cairnwell had repercussions. The leader of the Argyll MacDairmaids had left seven young sons behind him on this raid and they vowed revenge. Several tales survive about the MacDairmaids' seeking revenge but the superior cunning of Cam Ruadh triumphed – until one year the Argyll lads decided to come after him in the middle of winter.

The story goes that Cam and his wife were sitting snug in their house while a vicious blizzard whirled outside. Mrs Grant said to her husband, 'What would you do, husband, if the Argyll men came after you on a night like this?'

'I would let them in by the fire and give them meat.'

'And then what would you be doing?' she asked.

'I think I would let them sleep through the worst of the storm.'

'And what then?'

'Och, I would let them be gone once the storm had passed.'

'Be as good as your word then,' came a gruff and quivering voice from outside, 'for we are close to death out here.'

'Surrender your arms first,' shouted Cam Ruadh, grabbing his sword and dirk and standing beside the door, back to the wall.

'Send your wife to the door and we will give her our weapons,' came the voice.

Mrs Grant went and opened the door and one by one the near-frozen MacDiarmaids handed over their weapons. A couple of them had to be carried by their brothers and the miserable group huddled round the roaring fire with hardly a glance at their intended victim. A sheep was butchered and put into the pot while the unexpected visitors were given bannocks and cheese, washed down with a bladder full of whisky. When the sheep was cooked all were fed and allowed to stay until the blizzard blew itself out. Having taken meat under Cam's roof the MacDiarmaids were under the obligations of hospitality and could do no harm to their host. Furthermore, so taken were they by his generosity and the realisation that he could have left them outside to die that the MacDiarmaids declared an end to the feud. In fact, they swore a bond of friendship and in future years were able to call upon the great military skills of Cam Ruadh in battles back in Argyll.

Ledenhendrie

The traditional cattle-raiding of the Highland warriors was usually carried out on long autumn nights when the moon was full. There was no point in raiding a nearby clan – that would be too obvious and would lead to all-out war. Far better to show your mettle by raiding a good distance away where, if you were skilful enough, you might come back with a substantial haul. Such raiding was so central to the Highland way of life that there were set amounts to be paid for crossing other clans' lands with lifted cattle. In some cases these fees would ensure that the beneficiaries would refuse to let any pursuers chase raiders over their land.

By the seventeenth and eighteenth centuries Highland society was in decline and raids were beginning to be carried out in the Lowlands and as far away as Galloway. It seems likely that this type of activity had been an intrinsic part of society for centuries.

Year after year, raiders would follow established routes to prey on clans who in turn would attempt to prey on them. The routes in many instances are similar to the later drove roads, although the necessity for hiding from followers would take the reivers into more difficult and sheltered terrain. One route used by the Lochaber men for centuries was known as *Rathad nam Mearlaich*, or thieves' road, which name is perhaps not that old. The route came from Lochaber through Rothiemurchus, along the south side of the lovely Loch Morlich (B31), through the pass of Lochan Uaine (B30) by Loch Gamhna, then along the south side of Loch an

Eilean (B32), then east into the hills. This route was extensively used at different times by men from the MacPherson, Cameron and MacIntosh clans and others from Badenoch and Strathspey.

In the lonely hills between Glen Clova and Glenesk there is an unassuming ridge overlooking the Water of Saughs (D6) called the Shank of Donald Young. This name commemorates a battle between raiders from Braemar and the men of Fern in Strathmore sometime around the beginning of the eighteenth century. The raiders had come into Strathmore and lifted all the cattle and other beasts around Fern, a wee village on the braes of Angus, about ten kilometres north of Forfar. As usual the raid took place in the dark and the raiders drove their booty up through Glen Lethnot (D7) and along the Water of Saughs, heading back towards Deeside. At dawn the loss was discovered and all the men from the surrounding area came into the village. Not all were keen to pursue the raiders, who were surely heavily armed and used to battle – most of the Fern men were farmers or crofters and had not been brought up to fight. Still, a couple of local men were keen on preserving Highland warrior traditions and gave the lead.

These men were James Winter, whose descendants lived on the braes of Angus until recently and James MacIntosh, better known as Ledenhendrie, the name of his farm, east of Fern. Both were skilled swordsmen and soon rallied a sufficient number of men, some equipped with firearms, to start the pursuit. A few hours later they caught up with the raiders two or three kilometres beyond Blackhaugh at the head of Glen Lethnot. As they neared the men driving the cattle, most of the raiders turned and came towards the Fern men, led by a veritable giant of a man. This was a weel-kennt reiver who had adopted the name of one of history's most notorious cattle-lifters, the Halkit Stirk. This is Scots for 'white-faced steer'.

The two sides faced each other and the giant issued a challenge that he would fight their best swordsman, and the winner take all. Both Ledenhendrie and Winter felt themselves bound by the code of Highland honour and Ledenhendrie accepted the challenge. The two men were not long fighting when it became obvious that the reiver had more than a height and reach advantage. He was also a very fine swordsman and laughingly sliced the buttons of MacIntosh's coat, calling on him to yield. Ledenhendrie was nothing if not courageous and would not surrender.

The two groups faced each other over open ground, the two swordsmen half way between them. Suddenly a hare started from the heather in front of the Fern men and made a beeline for the Highlanders. One of them immediately shouted (in Gaelic): 'It's a witch! They're using witchcraft!'

Ledenhendrie

Putting his gun to his shoulder, he fired at the speeding animal. He missed, but the Fern men, thinking he was breaking the agreement, immediately started to return fire. As the Fern men outnumbered the raiders by more than two-to-one, they soon had the better of the fight. Winter hamstrung the giant from behind but he continued fighting on his knees until he was killed by Ledenhendrie. Only the few Deeside men who had stayed with the cattle escaped. The cattle were recaptured. Of the Fern men only one, Donald Young, was killed and the ridge above where he died was given his name.

CHAPTER 4

The Turn of the Seasons

SCOTLAND STILL HAS FIRE rituals whose origins go back further than we know. The Burnin o the Clavie at Burghead (B21), the fireballs at Stonehaven (B46) and the dramatic Up-Hellya Festival in Shetland (B8) all celebrate the new year. In the past, however, there were many other seasons when the use of fire was central to ritual.

Beltane

Midsummer Day, or St John's Day, was accompanied by bonfires, as were the two main festivals of the ancient agricultural year, Beltane and Samhain. These two festivals were the pivots of the year for most people in pre-industrial Britain. Beltane on 1 May was essentially a celebration of the summer and Samhain on 1 November was in some senses a feast of thanksgiving after the harvest was in. However there was much more to these great festivals and Beltane in particular has left many markers in the landscape.

Early commentators, misreading the first part of 'Beltane' interpreted it as a reference to the pagan Baal from the Bible. Others saw this central role of fire as a reference to a sun god – but things were hardly that simple.

In traditional Beltane celebrations, fires were lit on hilltops, which made them more visible. Several Scottish placenames mention fire for this reason. The dominating hill of Tinto (D64) in Lanarkshire was the site of the ancient fires, its earlier name Tintock deriving from Gaelic *teinteach*, fiery. There is another Tintock (C8) northeast of Glasgow. Carntyne (C6) derives from *carn teineadh*, or fire cairn, and between Teviotdale and Liddesdale is Needslaw, named after the neid-fire raised there. Another possible site name is

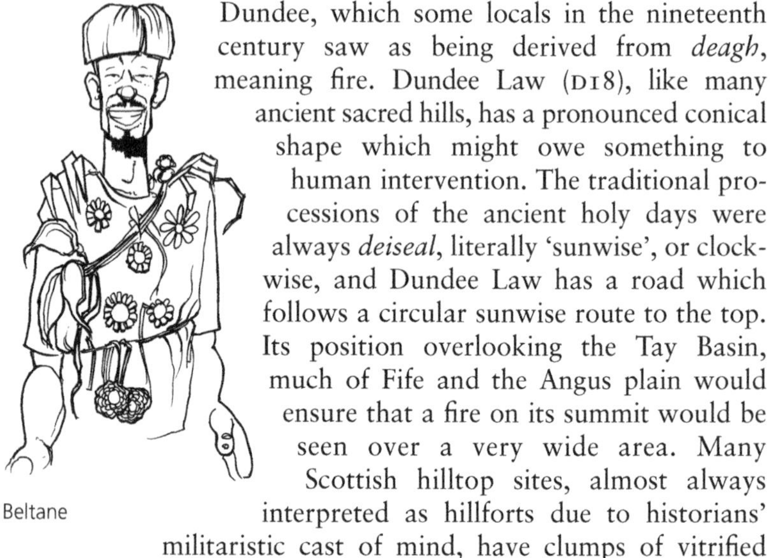
Beltane

Dundee, which some locals in the nineteenth century saw as being derived from *deagh*, meaning fire. Dundee Law (D18), like many ancient sacred hills, has a pronounced conical shape which might owe something to human intervention. The traditional processions of the ancient holy days were always *deiseal*, literally 'sunwise', or clockwise, and Dundee Law has a road which follows a circular sunwise route to the top. Its position overlooking the Tay Basin, much of Fife and the Angus plain would ensure that a fire on its summit would be seen over a very wide area. Many Scottish hilltop sites, almost always interpreted as hillforts due to historians' militaristic cast of mind, have clumps of vitrified stone – stone melted together by extremely fierce heat. It is worth considering whether the use of such sites in quarterly fire rituals may have played a part.

In any case, it is certain that even into the nineteenth century many, if not most, parishes in Scotland seem to have had their own local, smaller hilltop sites for Beltane. One such place is Tully-belton (82) in Perthshire which does not have a particularly notable hill in the immediate area. Instead, Beltane fires were kindled at the circle of eight stones close by, just as was done at Calanais in Lewis and the Ring of Stenness in Orkney. Other places with obvious locations are Balquhidder (C15) and Killin (C16), both in Perthshire. At Balquhidder there is a small green conical hill which, like the one in Killin, known as *Tom nan Ainneal*, are quite likely to have been partially sculpted if not entirely raised by human hand. Even Iona, that example of Christian sanctity, has its *Cnoc nan Ainneal*, again meaning hill of fires. These neid-fires were created by friction because there could be no use of iron – flint and steel were prohibited. This is reminiscent of the avoiding of iron because the fairies 'disliked' it.

It was after the Beltane ceremony that cattle were taken to the high pastures to be fattened up, having been indoors for all of the winter and possibly much of the spring. (Today we tend to see things as either sacred or profane but in ancient times it is likely that such practicalities could easily be incorporated into practices we would see as primarily religious, or certainly spiritual. When one recalls that the Beltane fires were made in many cases from sacred woods which included such pungent materials as juniper, it could be there was an aspect of fumigation in this rite.)

Before the fire was ceremonially kindled, every hearth fire in the community was smoored. Once the main ceremonies were over each person would take a lighted piece of peat or a torch from the fire and return home. Then they would walk clockwise round their own lands and houses carrying the holy fire before entering the house to light the fire anew. This process of walking round the fields was known as saining. It combines the ideas of purification and sanctification – ensuring prosperity and good crops for the coming year.

The Beltane feast was a time for celebration which included the cooking of special foods. According to a report from Callander (C12) in the beautiful Trossachs, the Beltane ceremony was quite elaborate. The young men of each hamlet would meet on a hill and cut a round table in the ground, big enough for everyone involved to sit around it. They would make a fire and then a big dish of 'caudle' was made. This was a form of custard made from eggs and milk. They would also make the simple and delicious oatcakes known as bannocks. The Beltane bannock was special, however: it would be marked into portions, one for everyone in the company. Then one of these would be blackened with charcoal from the fire, the bannock broken into pieces and put into a bonnet or bag. The young men would all put on blindfolds and select a piece of bannock. The person who got the marked piece was then the 'devoted' one and made to jump three times through the flames. There is little doubt that this is an echo of a much earlier practice where the person chosen was actually sacrificed, quite probably by being burned alive. (Being chosen as a sacrificial victim was a great honour in ancient times.) And even more recently, there are hints in some reports that if anyone was injured or killed during the festivities of Beltane or Samhain that this, though regrettable, brought good luck for the coming year. (After all, good luck was the primary reason for these festivals – to ensure the continuing turn of the seasons and the health of the crops and animals.) In some areas the chosen person was known as the *cailleach bealltainn* and a great show would be made of pretending to throw the victim onto the fire.

Numbers were very important in the rituals and in most cases people would go three times round the fire. However, in some cases the number nine was of the greatest significance. In some Highland districts the raising of the neid-fire involved the number nine. A well-seasoned plank of oak would be bored through, into which hole would be placed a wimble or bore of the same wood. Sometimes a frame would be erected and in the middle an axle-tree would be fitted. Then nine people would turn it at a time. Sometimes as many as eighty-one people would be involved. The turning of the wimble in the wood, through the use of an axle-tree or not, created friction which caused heat, eventually raising a flame which would be fed with tinder to achieve a good fire. It was believed in most areas that if any of those turning the wood for the neid-fire were guilty of a serious crime then the fire would not start. As all the fires in the area or parish would have been smothered before the ceremony, it was vitally important that the ritual was successful. Until the nineteenth century certain local families were known for being 'of the stones' and tradition says that they had the duty of raising the neid-fire at the Beltane ceremonies held there.

It seems likely that this aspect of the ceremonies arose after the witch persecutions of the sixteenth and seventeenth centuries, while the rest of the rites come from much earlier.

Many of the customs associated with Beltane such as 'maying' – going to the woods to collect greenery – were not concerned with fertility in the abstract alone. This was customarily the time for a great deal of sexual activity.

Beltane feasts seem to have persisted longest in rural districts but it is in the city that they are being revived. For several years now the Beltane fires have blazed again on Calton Hill (as discussed above) and they have found an echo in various other places in

Scotland. The displacement of the Samhain fire feast to Guy Fawkes Night has kept certain aspects of that ancient feast of the dead alive.

On the south side of Kinnoull Hill (D23), Perth, overlooking the River Tay, there is a small cave known as the Dragon's Hole. This was the site of a particular Beltane rite until the end of the sixteenth century. An eyewitness account from 1559 tells of a strange flower-bedecked man standing at the cave entrance and repelling a series of young men who came up the hill to struggle with him. This rite drew virtually the entire populace from Perth and the eyewitness was told it commemorated the battle between St Serf and a dragon (which had preyed on the local lassies until the saint killed it). After the Reformation it took many years for the local presbytery to stop people going to celebrate this rite. There are records of fines being levied on such people and even today there are hearts scratched on the walls of the cave, suggesting that the link with fertility has not quite gone.

Samhain

Samhain is the polar opposite of Beltane. Where Beltane is a feast of supplication, Samhain is in many ways a feast of thanksgiving. However, it does have a sense of ancestor worship and echoes of a cult of the dead.

The rituals of Halloween might go as far back in time as the Stone Age when the great chambered cairns of Scotland were built. People held on to these ancient beliefs to such an extent that in 835 the Church moved the Feast of All Saints from 21 February to 31 October to try and counteract the ancient pagan rituals. It did not work totally, however, as 2 November was consecrated in 998 as the Feast of All Souls, dedicated to the faithful dead of the Church.

All over Scotland the Samhain rites continued – and some still do. Around 1840 a Sheriff Barclay travelled from Dunkeld (D27) to Aberfeldy (D28) – no more than 16 kilometres – and saw at least 30 fires blazing on hill-tops. He said that each had people dancing around it.

As at Beltane many of the rituals of Halloween involved repeating actions three or nine times but at this time of the year much of the activity centred round divination. While in ancient times this probably was a very serious business indeed, by historical times much of what was done had more to do with affairs of the heart than anything else.

Many of the sites of the Beltane fires were also used at Samhain as, for example, Calton Hill. Here the hazel trees which give the hill its name provided nuts which were used in the divination process. Two nuts would be placed on a shovel in the fire and if they jumped together this was a sign of good fortune in love, while if they jumped apart it signified heartbreak. Such was the extent of this practice that another name for Samhain or Halloween was Nutcrack Night.

Again, as at Beltane, special foods were prepared for Halloween. A very strange rite concerning the Halloween bannock used to take place just before Halloween in Rutherglen (C5) as late as the early nineteenth century.

The basic bannock was a sour type of cake whose dough had to be started over a week before they were needed. A group of six or eight women would gather in one house and mark out a sacred space in which to carry out their duties. There they would sit in a circle round the fire, each of them with a baking board on her knees. The leading figure was given the name Bride and the rest were designated her maidens. Two other women were called Hodler and Todler, the former on the eastern side of Bride, the latter on her other side. Todler would start by taking a small piece of the fermented dough and fashioning it into a bannock. She would pass it on to the person sitting next to her 'sunwise', or clockwise, who would work it more – and so it would go until the bannock was smooth and wafer thin at which point Bride would bake it on a griddle over the fire. The sitting in a circle, the passing of the bannock sunwise and the designation 'Bride' suggest a very old idea indeed. We recall that it is at Halloween that Bride, the Goddess of Summer, ends her reign and is replaced by the Cailleach, the Goddess of Winter.

In many parts of the country well into this century the idea of

Halloween fire was closely linked to the idea of witches. Young men in rural areas would go round the houses asking for peat to burn the witches. After dark the young folk would run around the fires shouting, 'Fire, fire. Burn the witches!' When the fires eventually died down the ashes would be scattered over a wide area to scare off all evil spirits – and incidentally to help fertilise the fields. When the last spark died, the gathered throng scattered with cries of 'Deil tak the hindmaist,' or even, 'The cutty black sow wantin a tail, tak the hindmaist!' (This might be a faded echo of the old association of the sow with goddess figures, noted by scholars. The association was always a dark one.)

Then the ashes of the fire would be laid out in the form of a circle and everyone present would place a stone round the edge of the circle. Whoever's stone was gone in the morning would not be expected to live out the year.

Samhain

Witch-burning survived at Balmoral (B45) and Queen Victoria herself was supposed to have greatly enjoyed the spectacle. Here a figure of a witch called the Shandy Dann was brought to a great bonfire in a cart accompanied by pipers and others in traditional Highland dress. One brave soul would actually be in the cart with the dummy. As the procession came near the fire those pushing it would speed up, racing by the time they got there. Suddenly they would stop a few paces away from the fire. An indictment of the witch would be read out. Then, to the sound of skirling pipes, the cart would be rushed into the bonfire and tipped into it, the occupant of the cart leaping clear at the last possible moment. Like many of the rites of Halloween there seems to be some sort of memory of human sacrifice in this peculiar practice.

One of the trademarks of Halloween is, of course, dressing up. Although this has now been superceded by the commercial practise of 'trick or treat', the tradition of guising at Halloween was originally more than just children having a laugh.

The idea of guising was to make oneself unrecognisable. It often involved cross-dressing. Guisers may have originated as pagan priests who represented the spirits of the dead. But ultimately, the disguise was to protect oneself from the attentions of the spirits who were believed to be abroad on the night as much as to provide a cover for mischief. It was long believed that the gap between the world of the living and the world of the dead shrank on Halloween when the dead and all sorts of spirits walk the earth.

The use of neep-lanterns (lanterns made from turnips) is traditional in Scotland, as opposed to pumpkins. Turnips introduce a haunting skull shape. This may hark back to the warrior tradition of collecting the skulls of enemies slain in battle. We know also that skulls were once used to decorate temples throughout Europe. And in Scotland there are wells all over with legends of people being beheaded and their heads then being washed there.

There are quite a few of these wells in Skye and even a *Loch nan Ceann*, loch of the heads, near Cuidrach (A18) in the Trotternish area of Skye. The story here is that in a battle between MacDonalds and MacLeods the former were totally victorious, killing all their enemies. They then cut their heads off and rolled them down a hill into the loch. As the heads rolled down the hill they were said to have called '*Theb, theab a latha dhol leinn,*' – 'Almost, we almost won the day'. Many scholars see the idea of a head cult as in some way essentially Celtic but we should remember that in Norse mythology Odin himself cuts off the head of the giant Mimir, cures it in herbs and keeps it in Mimir's Well at the foot of the world-tree Yggdrasil.

An old name for the Halloween fire was 'shannack' and the night itself was sometimes known as Shannack Night. The term comes from Gaelic *samhnach* and survives in some placenames as, for example, Shannacher, near Fowlis Wester (D34), a wee village just east of Crieff in Strathearn. Here the link with the distant past is manifestly clear in the landscape. In and around Fowlis Wester there are standing stones, a stone circle, a Pictish cross-slab and an old kirk, showing the continuous use of the area as a focus for religious behaviour from pagan through to Christian times. Our ancestors found certain places particularly well suited to religious observance and it is remarkable how many such sites still attract worshippers today.

Again a very wide spread practice was the raising of bonfires at Midsummer, renamed St John's Day in Christian times. The summer solstice has long been seen as a special day in most societies. So, too, in Durris (B47) on the river Dee near Banchory where the fires were lit on Cairnshee, the cairn of the fairies, and were supported by a bequest from a local man who left money for the local herd-boys to continue this festive rite.

CHAPTER 5

Saints

IT WAS DELIBERATE Christian policy to take over pagan sanctuaries and build churches there as Pope Gregory wrote in the seventh century: 'In this way we hope that all the people, seeing that their temples are not destroyed, may abandon their error and, flocking more readily to their accustomed resorts, may come to know and adore the true God.' Churches are commonly found on top of mounds today, as St Vigean's (D12) at the edge of Arbroath. The overlap of pagan and Christian continued with religious leaders.

Scotland has many saints who do not figure in the official lists. Some do, of course, like Columba – but even he is associated with behaviour and attributes that hardly suggest Christian devotion. Some of our saints like St Brigit are clearly christianised versions of earlier pagan figures and yet others like St Kentigern seem to bridge the gap between pagan and Christian. There are saints who slay dragons in what might be allegories of the conquering of pagan belief, saints whose association with ancient holy wells helped to perpetuate the functioning of such sites and still other saints who seem to be pagan ambassadors.

The function of these saints' Lives seems to have been to convince people that the priests of the Church were more than a match for the pagan priests or druids who preceded them.

St Serf

St Serf or St Servanus, as he was also called, is a mysterious figure. Of the many miracles attributed to him, one has it that he threw his pastoral staff across the River Forth from his cell at Culross (D38) and when it landed it took root and blossomed into an apple tree. Given the Celtic idea of Avalon (the Island of Apples) where Morgan took the wounded Arthur to be tended by her and her eight sisters, this idea is suggestive.

Serf

What St Serf is best known for, however, is his dragon-slaying. At Dunning in Strathearn he killed a dragon and is said to have done the same thing at the Dragon's Cave on the south side of Kinnoull Hill, Perth. He had been summoned to rid the countryside of the dragon that had been seizing maidens and taking them to his lair to devour them. This was the event said to be celebrated at the Dragon's Cave on Beltane up to the Reformation and beyond. This celebration obviously had to do with fertility. The eyewitness account we have describes the main participant being bedecked in flowers and greenery. This finds an echo in the festival of St Serf which used to take place in Culross on 1 July. This involved the carrying of tree branches and flowers as well as sacred relics and was accompanied by dancing and other revelry. The minute-book of the local kirk-session at Perth refers to 'heathenish practices' and describes young men and women marching to the Dragon's Hole with pipes and drums. They persisted for at least 20 years after the Reformation. In the cave mentioned above, there are hearts carved on the walls still – some traditions just quietly live on!

St Serf is also associated with the Culdees, successors of the Celtic church who practised alongside their Roman brethren in many of our great cathedrals into the Middle Ages. It was in his supposed capacity as a Culdee that Serf was given the large flat island in Loch Leven (D39) that still bears his name. Although he has wells and churches dedicated to him from Culross to Dunning and Dysart (D53), near Kirkcaldy, there is no real suggestion of when he lived other than his involvement with another saint, Kentigern.

St Kentigern

Better known by the name Mungo, which was given him by St Serf, this early saint is a complex figure. As the patron saint of Glasgow he is especially associated with Glasgow Cathedral (C7). The Glasgow coat of arms shows a salmon and a ring that come from the best-known of his miracles.

St Mungo was at the court of the king of Strathclyde when the queen began to have an affair with one of the members of the court. Stupidly she gave him a ring which she had been given by the king himself. One day her lover was sound asleep by the side of the Clyde when the king came by and noticed the man wearing his ring. Carefully he slipped it from the sleeper's finger and threw it far out into the Clyde. Returning to the court he publicly asked the queen to bring him the ring he had given her. She immediately went to Kentigern to ask him what to do. He told her to send her handmaiden to the river with a net and bring back a salmon. The queen ordered this done and when the handmaiden returned with a salmon, Kentigern cut open the fish and there in its belly was the ring. The queen at once cleaned it and took it to her husband, who was forced to accept her pleas of innocence.

This looks suspiciously like a priest condoning adultery, but it may simply be a christianized version of an older story. For Kentigern seems to belong to an older world even though he is said to have met Columba (who came to Scotland from Ireland in 563). Kentigern's mother was Thenaw, daughter of King Loth of the Lothians. In the Arthurian romances he is portrayed as King Arthur's brother-in-law, and father of both Mordred and Gawain. Loth's capital was on Traprain Law, the massive hill that rises from the plain of East Lothian near Haddington (D5), the historical home of the Celtic tribe the Romans called Votadini.

Kentigern's mother, Thenaw, was a devoutly Christian young woman who was determined to take a vow of chastity. Because of her innocence of all worldly matters she was seduced by a visiting prince who was young enough not to have yet grown a beard and passed himself off initially as a girl. Finding herself pregnant, the young girl informed her father. He flew into a rage but said it would all be made well if she married the beardless youth. She refused and in his anger the king then demanded she marry a lowly shepherd. When she refused yet again he ordered her to be put into a chariot and rolled off the top of Traprain Law. As the chariot went over the edge the maiden began to pray and instead of plummeting like a stone the chariot began to float gently downwards. This only served to make Loth even angrier and he decided she should be put to sea in a coracle with no oars. This was then done and she floated out on the tide into the Firth of Forth. Again she prayed and her coracle fetched up on the Isle of May (D52). From here she was accompanied by a vast shoal of fishes up the river and eventually landed at Culross on the northern bank of the Forth. Here she managed to light a fire and later gave birth to her son all alone. At that point St Serf came to investigate the light and finding the mother and child, the young Mungo / Kentigern, he took them into his community. Nothing more is told of Thenaw although St Enoch's bears a version of her name in Glasgow today.

Kentigern

Not only are St Mungo's antecedents straight from the oral tradition of Brythonnic-speaking Celtic tribes, some of the miracles attributed to him are redolent of magic and paganism. Perhaps due to the strangeness of his birth, Mungo was not popular with the other pupils of St Serf.

On one occasion it was his turn to sit by the fire to make sure it did not go out overnight, but he fell asleep. Some of the other boys came upon him and smothered the fire. When he awoke the boy was faced with a cold fire in mid-winter. So he gathered up some leaves, prayed and blew on them and they burst into flame. The leaves he used are said to have been from the hazel tree, one of the ancient sacred woods often used in the raising of the neid-fire.

Another time when his back was turned the other boys killed St Serf's pet robin. He took the creature into his hands, said a prayer over it, blew on it and it was alive. A while after this the community's cook died and Mungo's companions said he ought to be able to bring the cook back to life as he had already done so with the robin – either that or he would have to be cook. Mungo restored the cook to life. From then on St Serf was aware of the boy's abilities and began to love him deeply.

When at last Mungo decided it was time to strike out on his own St Serf was displeased and tried to stop him. Eventually the younger man managed to cross the Forth and when he saw his mentor approaching a boat on the other side of the river, he summoned up a storm to prevent St Serf crossing after him. After this Mungo met an old pagan who said he had foreseen that he would meet a great saint and be converted to Christianity before dying. So Mungo baptised the old man and he promptly died. Mungo put the body on a cart drawn by oxen and decided that he would found his first church where the beasts stopped. This they eventually did by the Molendinar burn. He built a simple wooden structure on the site of what is now Glasgow Cathedral.

For a while Mungo was forced to go and live in Wales. The story goes that he chose the site of his church there by following a wild boar. The boar, of course, figures strongly in the ancient legends of the Celtic-speaking peoples and is a strong pagan symbol.

In all of the stories of St Mungo he seems quite unlike what we tend to believe early missionary saints were like – he indulges in magic and weather-raising and when he has come to the court of the King of Strathclyde he actively protects an adulterous queen. Of course, early saints' Lives from all over Europe are full of magical twists and turns. Whoever or whatever Kentigern initially was, it seems at least a possibility that he is one of those figures from the far pagan past recreated in Christian times.

St Maelruba

Opposite the Isle of Raasay (A25) on the coast of Wester Ross is the tiny village of Applecross (A31). This quaintly named settlement has nothing to do with apples. Rather, it is an old, probably Pictish name, *Apur-Crossan*, meaning the mouth of the Crossan, the local burn. It is associated with a saint who has been the cause of much speculation, St Maelruba. Placenames associated with him are various. Loch Maree (A32) and its island Eilean Maree, 25 kilometres to the northeast, are believed to be named for him. So was Amulree (D30), north of Crieff, and it is his fair that was celebrated in Banff (B22) as the Summareve Fair. In the late seventeenth century divination rites were still being carried out in the saint's name in Easter Ross as was the well-known bull sacrifice on Eilean Maree, itself also known as St Mourie's Isle. The picture is further complicated by some commentators seeing the first element of his name, *mael* or *maol* as Gaelic for cropped or bald, in reference to his tonsure perhaps. The belief is that like most of the early Gaelic monks, he cut his hair from ear to ear and let it grow long at the back – a practice thought to have originated with the druids. (The traditional Christian tonsure left a ring of hair round the entire head, of course.) Whatever the origin of the name of this complex figure, local belief in the powers associated with him lasted a long time. Even in the mid-nineteenth century lunatics were taken to St Mourie's Isle to kneel before the weatherworn altar, drink from the sacred waters of the loch and then be dipped three times in the loch itself. The beneficent powers of the well were thought to be at their peak on the saint's day, 25 August. He was long referred to as the 'God Mourie'.

St Merchard

Another saint to whom supplications were made was St Merchard. He is believed to have been one of the first Christian missionaries to have come into the west central Highlands, although it is unclear whether he came as a follower of Columba or of the even earlier saint Ninian, said to have converted the Picts. He founded several churches in the Glenmoriston area (A30) on the west of the Great Glen. His main foundation was in Glenmoriston below the ancient hillfort of Dun Dreggan (A29) where the mighty Finn MacCool was said to have slain a dragon. On his death Merchard left instructions that his body was to be placed in an ox-cart and the oxen set moving.

Wherever they stopped, that was where he was to be buried. (This is the same method used by St Kentigern to locate his church.)

Like several other saints Merchard left a bell with miraculous powers behind him, kept in the church at Clachan Merchard. The bell had the power to ring of its own accord whenever a funeral approached the kirkyard. One dark night the locals were awakened in the middle of the night by Merchard's bell. Several of them headed at once to the kirkyard, where they found the body of a freshly-murdered man. The murderer was found nearby and subjected to the justice of the time – hanging.

The bell shared another feature with other Celtic bells: it could fly back to its home if removed. Whenever it was installed in a new church it would fly back to Clachan Merchard. At last in the seventeenth century the old church collapsed beyond repair and a new one had to be built some distance away. The bell was left on a tombstone in the original kirkyard where it remained for over a century until some unfortunate stole it. Despite this, Merchard himself lingered in the area a long time.

One of the clan laws that in some areas survived very late was the *each-ursainn*, the horse fine. This was a fine which the clan chief could levy on a family which had lost one of its male members. It was derived from the old clan obligation to fight on behalf of the clan when called on to do so by the chief. In this case, however, the fine – livestock to the value of a horse – was being levied on a distraught widow, long after the warrior function of the clansmen had ceased. The chief, MacPhatrick, sent his law-officer to do the dirty work of removing almost all the sheep that the widow had, leaving her effectively destitute. The woman prayed that night to St Merchard. The same night the law-officer was awakened by a thunderous voice which declared to him: 'I am great Merchard of the miracles, passing homeward in the night. Declare thou unto MacPhatrick that the widow's sheep will never bring him good.'

The terrified law-officer fell out of bed and ran to rouse his master and tell him what had happened. The sheep were returned to the widow and MacPhatrick never again tried to turn old clan law to his own advantage. Would that other lairds had been likewise restrained.

St Columba

St Columba is a figure of great importance in Scottish history, politically as well as religiously. He became important to Scotland partly because of something that happened in the seventh century. Columba's followers had clashed with mainstream Christian practise up until the Synod of Whitby in 664. The clashes had to do with practises in the early Gaelic church, mainly concerned with different tonsure and ways of calculating Easter. This continued even after Adomnán, abbot of Iona (A17), nominally accepted Roman practice, and thus the superiority of Rome at Whitby. (Adomnán was a kinsman of Columba and his most determined defender.) The ancient rites of the Columban Church were thus carried on for centuries in many of our leading cathedrals by those religious communities called Culdees, which existed alongside the official Roman Church into the early Middle Ages. Reference to this allowed the post-Reformation Church in Scotland to claim an earlier pedigree than the now despised Catholic Church.

Columba, however, was already a major personality in his own lifetime. A member of the Uí Néill dynastic family in Ulster, he probably had a right to be a king in Ireland himself but opted instead for the religious life.

One of the best-known stories concerning Columba involves plagiarism. Columba made a secret copy of a psalter belonging to another cleric without getting the owner's permission. This was considered a serious crime and at a special ecclesiastical court he was found guilty of transgressing the law and ordered to hand over the copy to the owner of the original. Columba refused to accept the judgement. He went further and called on his kinsmen to support him. The situation worsened and eventually a battle was fought in which many men died. After this Columba was sent into exile in Scotland with the instruction to convert at least as many new souls to Christianity as he had caused to be killed in the battle. This is how he came to Iona. Many laments attributed to the saint record his sadness at leaving Ireland.

Columba was also a noted bard and he spoke on behalf of the traditional rights of bards in Irish society at the Convention of

Drum Ceat in 575. The bards had originally been one of the druidic orders and Columba went so far as to call Christ his 'Druid' in one work. In another he refers to his greatest fear as the sound of an axe in 'the oak groves of Derry.' (*Doire Cholmchille* – the oak grove of Columba – is the full name of Derry today.)

On Iona there is a site called *Reilig Orain*, the burial place of Oran. This connects to the story of Columba arriving on the island and deciding that a human sacrifice was necessary to appease the spirits of Iona! One of his monks, Oran, offered himself as the sacrifice and was buried alive. Three days later Columba opened up the grave and found Oran was still alive. He told Columba that death was no marvel and Hell was not as it was said to be. The saint was greatly offended at this and ordered that the grave be filled in again. This suggests either a garbled version of some kind of initiation or possibly the very old tradition of burying a human in the foundations of a new building as a form of sacrifice.

While at the Pictish court in Inverness Columba was involved in a battle of magic with the king's druid, Broichan, in which control of the weather was one of the main areas of combat. The idea of the great Christian saint taking part in a battle of magic seems a bit strange today but back in the Dark Ages, and even into medieval times, such ideas were not unusual.

St Abban

The Isle of Jura is steeped in mythology and legend. It has its own goddess figure and a range of hills known as the Paps of Jura with three, not two, peaks. At its northern end is the great whirlpool Corryvreckan (C17), the legendary significance of which is discussed above. A goddess on Jura was said to protect her deer from any non-Jura hunters. Today its largely uninhabited northern end has vast herds of red deer. In such a location it is not surprising that the stories of early Christian figures should have suggested pagan belief patterns.

Such a one is St Abban who lived on the island with his grand-daughter. While out trying to catch fish, the old saint was washed off the rocks and drowned. The child somehow managed by herself and grew into a healthy young woman. One day while on the seashore collecting driftwood near where her grandfather had been swept away she inadvertently picked up a small piece of bone lying on the beach. At home she put the bone in with the kindling and later flung it with some of the driftwood onto the fire. Soon the bone was alight and a spark from it flew out and burned the girl. Nine months later St Abban was born again from the womb of his own grandchild. Here again we see the new faith dressing itself in old clothes to appeal more to the local inhabitants. A variant of this is the belief that it was dangerous for a virgin lass to touch either a bone or a dead body in case she became pregnant. It may also be an answer to why the water used to wash a corpse had to be poured over a stone securely fixed in the earth and capable of absorbing its force.

CHAPTER 6

Supernatural Beings

SCOTLAND IS LIKE ALL OTHER lands in that our traditions have many stories about supernatural beings, friendly and otherwise. In Chapter 1 we saw some of the tales associated with fairies but there are many more supernatural beings. There are wondrous waterhorses called kelpies, those strange sea-creatures, the silkies, who could take human or seal form, domestic spirits like the brownies and gruagachs and the truly mysterious Nessie, who many still believe in.

Nessie

Loch Ness is a fitting location for a mystery. This great body of water is over 30 kilometres long and has storms that are almost as bad as those at sea. Its origin is itself the subject of legend but for many centuries it has been best known for its mythological

Nessie

inhabitant, Nessie. Nowadays the monster of Loch Ness (generally considered to be female) is looked on without fear or horror but in her first recorded appearance she is a truly frightening creature.

According to Adomnán's Life of Columba the saint was on his way to Inverness when he and his companions came to the banks of the River Ness. They came across a group of men burying one of their number who had been killed by a water monster in the river. Spotting a boat on the far side of the river, Columba sent one of his monks to swim over for the boat. Just as the monk reached midstream a great monster arose out of the river, gave a great roar and bore down on the unfortunate man. The creature was within a few feet of the monk when Columba raised his hand and commanded the monster to stop. The monster reared back in terror, turned and fled back into the waters of the river. The monk swam to the other shore and got the boat to ferry his companions across. The watching locals were mightily impressed and thereafter had a great respect for the 'God of the Christians'. Whether or not this is just another instance of a saint's miracle it is intriguing that there have never been any stories of Nessie attacking a human since!

Kelpies

Another type of water-creature known all over Scotland is the kelpie, *each-uisge* or water horse. Although its form was usually that of a horse, the kelpie had the ability to change its shape and often appeared as a handsome young man and occasionally as a bonnie young woman. The kelpie's intent was almost always to lure its victims into the river and drown them and this may be an idea that originated from the dangers presented in trying to cross rivers in the long years before bridges were built. Most kelpies are said to have magnificent bridles which have magic powers themselves and anyone lucky enough to find a kelpie's bridle would be able to see all the invisible beings that populate our atmosphere by looking through the eyelets of the bridle.

Loch Slochd

One time in the not-so-distant past Seumas McGregor was on his way from Inverness to Glenlivet. He had made it as far as Loch Slochd (B25) when he had to rest. He was sitting thinking he should have made the journey on horseback when suddenly his own horse appeared in front of him, saddled, bridled and waiting to be mounted. Hardly thinking, Seumas climbed up on the horse's back and off he set eastward. They had hardly gone more than a short distance when the horse began veering towards the loch. At once Seumas realised what was happening: he had got on a kelpie's back! At once he cried out the name of the Trinity. The horse reared up and threw its rider, then dashed into the loch. Seumas was knocked out. When he awoke he found himself lying on the path with the kelpie's bridle firmly clasped in his hands. This bridle was said to be in the possession of a local man called Warlock Willie in Gaulrig, Banffshire, last century, and has since been used to help many people.

Not all who met kelpies escaped so lightly. Near the Bridge of Luib on the River Don is a boulder known locally as the Kelpie's Stane. One day a man came to the crossing point on the way to the funeral of a dead cousin. There had been torrential rain a few days earlier and the bridge had been carried away as the river flooded. Just as he was thinking of turning back a tall man appeared and said he would carry him to the other side. With the thought of his cousin's funeral bearing heavily on his mind, the traveller accepted the offer. As they reached the middle of the river the man whose shoulder he was sitting on turned into a fearsome horse. He had hitched a ride from a kelpie! Struggling furiously, the traveller managed to wrest himself from the kelpie's clutches and swim to the shore. The furious kelpie reared up and threw a massive boulder at him, which just missed him. This is the Kelpie's Stane. A similar tale is told of Shielhill Bridge near Memus (D9) in Angus and here the stone bears the mark of a kelpie's cloven hoof.

Loch Pityoulish

A tale is told of the kelpie that inhabited Loch Pityoulish (B28) near the River Spey in the foothills of the Grampian Mountains.

A group of young lads including the heir of Kincardine were playing by the loch. Suddenly a lovely black horse with a beautiful silver harness and richly carved saddle trotted along the bank towards them. The horse came right up to the boys and bowed its head as if to ask the boys to climb on its back. Immediately some of them climbed on its back while others stroked its bridle and its mane. Suddenly young Kincardine realised his hand was stuck to the horse's mane. This was no horse, he realised, just as the creature reared up and leapt into the loch. Into the waters it crashed, dragging the young lads down to the depths. Young Kincardine was stuck fast to its mane but he knew what he had to do. As they sank ever deeper he pulled out his dirk with his free hand and without hesitation he sliced off the fingers attached to the mane. He floated free and swam to the surface trailing blood as his companions were drowned in the dark waters of the loch. He had lost the fingers of one hand, but his quick-thinking had saved his life.

Loch nan Dubrachan

Loch nan Dubrachan in Skye is another body of water with a kelpie. One of the stories associated with it is that the kelpie there decided to live as a human for a while. Like all its kind the creature was handsome as a man, dark-haired and well-built as well. As is the way of such things, the handsome young man took the fancy of a local lass called Morag and before too long the couple were married. In the fullness of time a child was born. Morag was aware that her husband sometimes went off on his own for what she thought were long walks by the loch shore. One night, after he had been on one of these walks she looked closely at him lying sleeping beside her and started back in horror. There among the dark curled hair on his chest was sand! She knew then that this was no man, but a kelpie. Raising the bedclothes gently she slipped form the bed, dressed, wrapped her child in a blanket and fled from the house, never to return. It was said that for many years the kelpie could be heard in Loch nan Dubhrachan (A28) singing a sad song of his loneliness and wishing for the return of his Morag.

A Female Kelpie

Near Trotternish, also on Skye, there was another legendary kelpie. A bunch of young lasses were up at the shielings on Shadowy Hill one evening looking after the cattle. When they had lain down to sleep on the big communal bed of bracken and heather, they heard a quavering voice outside the bothy door asking to be let in. They looked to see who it was, and there was a little old woman who said she had lost her way. They let her in and said she could share their bed. The frail old woman said she was frightened of sleeping at the foot of the bed or at the back of the bed. The upshot was that the lasses, feeling sorry for her, let her sleep in the middle of them. The lass sleeping nearest the door of the bothy noticed that the old woman was restless and that she seemed to sleep only in bursts. Just as she herself was drifting off, she sensed the old woman moving about and turned to look. There she saw a terrible sight: the old woman had crawled right up next to one of the girls and had fastened her teeth in her arm. Screaming, the lass watching got up and made for the door. She wrenched the door open and ran as quickly as she could. Down the hillside she ran, pursued by the kelpie. She came to a stream near the church of Bracadale (A19) and just as the cock crew in nearby Balgowan, the maiden leapt over the stream. The kelpie could not cross the stream and, seeing its prey escape moaned, '*Duilich e, duilich e, alltan*,' meaning, 'Sad it is, sad it is, little streamlet'. Ever since then the burn has been known as the Alltan Duilich.

Silkies

Kelpies are not the only shape-shifting water-creature that can assume human guise. There is also the silkie, a sea-creature half seal and half human, stories of which are known through the Outer Hebrides and the northern archipelagos of Orkney and Shetland. One of the best known of the silkies is the hero of the great Scots ballad 'The Silkie of Sule Skerrie' which is a rocky isle about 40 kilometres west of Orkney. In one verse the silkie says

> I am a man upon the land,
> An I am a silkie in the sea,
> An when I'm far an far frae land,
> My hame it is in Sule Skerrie.

This ballad tells a tragic tale with its haunting tune: the silkie has a son by a human lass who goes on to marry a gunner. The silkie comes to her in a dream and foretells the gunner will kill him, which comes to pass.

This is something all of silkie tales have in common – they are always sad. Some feature men with silkie wives whom they captured by getting hold of their skins while the silkies were in human

Silkies

form. Such silkie-women bore them children and were good mothers and wives but their seal skins had to be kept hidden or they would slip into them and return to their home below the waves, abandoning husband and children.

The Clan MacCodrum from North Uist (A10) are said to be descended from silkies. The belief is very ancient and linked to the idea that the silkies were attendants of the King of Lochlann, a magical kingdom which, initially an Otherworld location, became identified with Norway. Perhaps the seals were the totem of the MacCodrums in times gone by, for they would never do any harm to a seal.

Once there was a man who made his living from fishing and catching seals in the north of Scotland near John o Groats (B4). One day when he was out walking he saw a massive bull seal lying on a rock ahead of him. He ducked down and crept closer. When he was a few feet from the great beast he drew out his knife and leapt out to stab the creature. Up it reared, knocking him back off his feet and in an instant it had fled into the water taking his good knife with it. He was disappointed but soon forgot all about it. A few weeks later, late in the evening a dark stranger came to his door. The stranger was mounted on a black mare with grey mane and tail. He told the fisherman that his master wanted to do business with him; he should get on his horse and follow. The fisherman told him he had no horse, and the stranger offered to take him up behind him. The fisherman, intrigued by the obvious wealth of the stranger, was happy to go along and meet the man's master. At once they took off and the horse went like the wind. Soon they were standing on the cliffs overlooking the Pentland Firth. Puzzled, the fisherman asked where they were going and at that the horseman galloped forward. The three of them soared out into the air and crashed into the sea hundreds of feet below. Deeper and deeper they went but the fisherman could see everything around him and seemed to have no trouble breathing. After a while the horseman lifted his arm and pointed. There in the distance was a great white palace on the sea bed. They came near the magnificent building and all around them were seal-folk – men, women and children – all weeping. At last they were at the palace and entered through its great green doors. He was taken through many rooms until they came to a dimly lit chamber where a great seal lay stretched on a bed, moaning in pain. As the fisherman approached he saw a blood-stained knife on a small table by the bed. Looking closer he recognised his own knife. His guide then spoke and told him this was the King of the Seals, his own father, and he was dying. The horseman asked his pardon for deceiving him but he had had no alternative.

'It is I who need pardon from you for what I have done to your father,' said the fisherman.

'Lay your hand on the wound,' said his guide.

Doing so, the fisherman was amazed to see the wound heal over immediately. The great old seal rose up and thanked him.

Before they would let the fisherman go he was asked to swear that he would never hunt seals again and once he had done so he was assured that whenever he cast his nets in future he would always get a good catch. The great, grey seal bade him farewell and, mounted once again behind his guide, the fishermen was returned to his home. When he had dismounted, the Seal King's son once more thanked him and handed him a small leather bag before wheeling his horse round and disappearing at a great speed. The fishermen went in to his wife and told her all that had happened and when he opened the bag he found it full of beautiful pure-white pearls.

Not all supernatural beings are necessarily evil as the above story shows. Tradition has preserved tales of many other supernatural creatures who are actively beneficial to humankind.

Urisks

On the northern slopes of Ben Venue (C13) overlooking Loch Katrine in the Trossachs is *Coire nan Urisgean*. A *coire*, or corry, is a bowl-shaped depression on a mountain or hill, though in some cases its meaning explicitly suggests 'cauldron'. This particular corry is said to be where all the urisks of Scotland would gather.

The urisks were said to be a race of forest-dwelling spirits with long hair, long teeth and claws, and were half human, half goat. They were shy creatures, haunting the high mountain tops and deep woods of the Highlands. Initially they were believed to have been hostile to humans but over the years, like other spirits, some of them became attached to human families. The house of Tullochgorm (B29) in Strathspey had a pair of these creatures, male and female, the female being known as Mag Mulloch. She was said to be an excellent domestic servant but used to tell the mistress of the house of the misdeeds of other servants. She also had the interesting task of escorting the Laird of Tullochgorm when he was drunk. The name Mag Mulloch means 'hairy Meg', and this suggests a link to another form of spirit, the gruagach, whom we shall meet soon.

Brownies

Brownies were known for the help they gave. They were simple-seeming creatures, seldom to be seen during the day but active after nightfall when they would perform all sorts of domestic and agricultural tasks. While the urisks were traditionally associated with forests, the brownies were as common in the Lowland areas and the Northern Isles as in the Highlands. All of them, however, were extremely touchy.

About nine kilometres northeast of Moffat in the Borders is the farm of Bodesbeck (D62). Once the farm had a brownie who, like most of his kind, was shy but very hard-working. All he needed to keep going was some food and a libation of milk left out for him at night. Many of the brownies had their milk poured into a hollow in a stone from which they might lap it up.

The Brownie of Bodesbeck was very good at looking after the animals about the place and the farm prospered with his help. One year, the weather had been particularly fine and a spectacular harvest had been brought in. There were great celebrations that year and the farmer, thinking that the brownie should share in the general benefits he had helped so much to create, left out a special meal of a loaf of white bread and a jug of cream. The brownie came out that evening as usual but rather than being pleased, he was offended the farmer should think he needed extra consideration for working hard. He immediately left the farm, reputedly saying

Caa, brownie, caa,
Aa the luck o Bodesbeck,
Awa tae Leithen Ha.

Glaistigs and Gruagachs

Similar to the brownies were the glaistigs and gruagachs. The glaistig was generally associated with animals and dairying. Like the brownies, the glaistigs and the gruagachs liked milk, poured into hollows in stones. In Skye such stones were referred to as gruagach stones. These are reminiscent of the Stone Age cup-and ring-marks found all over Scotland and Ireland. On the misty Isle of Skye are standing stones which used to be known as gruagach stones, to which islanders used to bring milk libations. Some see the pouring of libations as an echo of ancient religious practice.

The name gruagach seems to mean long-haired one. Some scholars have noted that the name is very like that of the grach, druidesses who lived on the Isle of Sena off the Brittany coast in ancient times. The name may be related to Welsh *gwrach*, meaning hag or witch. The term survived into the nineteenth century in Pembrokeshire where the last sheaf of the harvest was called *gwrach*, exactly as the last sheaf in Scotland was called the *cailleach* in Gaelic-speaking areas. A similar term for a local goddess survived in mainland Brittany into the eighteenth century. The association with the harvest and the close match of the words suggests that the names might once have been an allusion to a Mother Goddess.

A Lochaber Glaistig

A story is told in Lochaber of a glaistig who was a form of water-spirit. She haunted rivers and lochs and was always ready to cause trouble. One time she set upon a horseman returning home to

The Lochaber Glaistig

Lianachan in the dead of night. This was a man known as Big Kennedy who was not one to be trifled with in any way. As she attacked him he grabbed her and, sitting her in front of him, he tied her to him with his sword belt. He headed home knowing he had been in danger of his life and that he would have to take drastic action. He kept her in his house overnight and at daybreak he heated the coulter of his plough in the kitchen fire until it was red hot. He then made the glaistig swear on the hot iron that never again would she plague the people of Lochaber while the sun shone by day or the moon by night. In doing this the glaistig burned her hand to the bone and leapt out of the window with a great shriek. She ran to a nearby hillock where she ejected three surges of blood. With each she cursed Big Kennedy and his seed forever. The hillock bore the scars ever since: where her blood poured the vegetation has been stained.

An Argyll Glaistig

In Glen Duror (A22) there was for a long time a glaistig who thought it her particular duty to prevent calves from suckling their mothers during the night.

When new tenants moved into the farm, they neglected to put out a libation for the glaistig. The following morning not a drop of milk was to be had from any cow. The situation was remedied that night and the following day things were back to normal.

Soon after this a new lass came to work on the farm. She was told to tend to the glaistig's needs, but she laughed at the very idea. That evening she went to the stream to fill a pail of water. As she knelt she got a great thump to her cheek which twisted her head half round. Try as she could, she could not move her head; it remained in a strange and twisted position. But despite all her tears nothing could be done and the next night she went to the stream again for water. As she knelt, fearful of what might happen next, she received another thump. This time it came form the other side and her head was restored to its rightful position. Here was a spirit with a mischievous sense of humour! When the farm was vacated, she stayed on and was rumoured to still be there in 1870.

CHAPTER 7

Witches and Warlocks

THE BEST-KENNT WITCH in Scotland is without doubt Cutty Sark from Burns's 'Tam o Shanter'. The hero is attracted to the sight of her firm young thighs and she is generally contrasted with the prevailing notion of a witch in Burns's day. What were witches meant to be like? An aged crone, an outcast possessed of so much power that people refuse her nothing? This popular notion combines nineteenth-century Gothicism and Hollywood simplicity, but it captures none of the controversy in perceptions of witches long ago.

Witch persecutions in Scotland, particularly in the aftermath of the Reformation in the late sixteenth century, were horrendous, vicious assaults. Usually 'witches' were old women rarely guilty of anything more than being friendless or utilising ancient cures that had come down through the centuries. However as the growth of masculine-dominated 'scientific' medicine began, these women were perhaps seen as an impediment to progress. In any case, Scotland's placenames are full of references to places where women were burned alive.

Various authors over the years have stressed the link between witches and a pagan religion that predated Christianity. Sacred sites often provide the link. Covens of witches are known to have gathered in kirkyards which themselves are often located on sites of pre-Christian sanctity such as at Auldearn (B17) in Moray and the Knock of Alves (B20) near Forres (B19). They also gathered on hilltops traditionally associated with the ancient fire festivals of Beltane (1 May) and Samhain (1 November) – also the main dates for the meetings of the witches themselves. These were the great feast days of the agricultural year (as discussed above) and were closely linked to fertility rites and other pagan practices. This does suggest some sort of continuity with the pagan past and it is more than likely that such cults had their own knowledge of healing as well as the more commonly stressed activities of working evil, prophesying and casting different kinds of spells.

A Spell on Eilean Maree

The use of spells to lift disease from both man and beast survived long after the advent of Christianity in Scotland. There is little doubt that much of what the reformed Church referred to as 'popish superstition' was in fact ancient religious or healing rituals. In 1678 it is recorded that Hector Mackenzie, his son and grandson sacrificed a bull for the recovery of Christine Mackenzie who was extremely ill. This occurred on the island of St Mourie in Loch Maree, Gairloch, mentioned in connection to St Maelruba, above. It seems the cure worked but the men were called before the local presbytery and censured for this act. Twenty years later there is mention of the same kind of activity associated with St Mourie's feast day in the district of Dingwall (B12) on the opposite coast.

Kate McNiven

To the north of the Strathearn town of Crieff (D35), long a centre of cattle trading, is the Knock of Crieff. This is an area abounding in legends. North of Knock is a standing stone, thought to be the remnant of a stone circle, known as Kate McNiven's Stane. Tradition tells that in 1583 Kate McNiven or Kate Nike Nieving was burned here. (The name Nike Nieving is clearly derived from the Gaelic *Nic Nevin*, meaning daughter of Nevin. In some sixteenth-century manuscripts Nike Nieving is said to be Queen of the Witches herself and there is a record of a notorious sorceress called *Nic Nevin* being burned in St Andrews in 1569.)

The name may also have been some sort of title, possibly within a witch cult of some kind. In Alexander Montgomerie's sixteenth-century poem 'The Flyting Betwixt Polwart and Montgomery', the name is given to the leading figure of all the Scottish witches. The story at Crieff is that Kate had been found guilty of witchcraft at a time when the paranoia against so-called witches was at its worst. In those dark days suspicion of witchcraft alone was often enough to condemn women to a nasty and sadistic death. Some versions of the story say she was burned on the Knock of Crieff itself just above the cliff face named after her, and others that she was burned below the cave in the north face of the Knock, now known as Kate McNiven's Cave. It is there that the unfortunate woman is said to have hidden from her pursuers until she was discovered. Wherever it may have happened, when she was captured she was tied up and surrounded by faggots. Just as the torch was lit a local laird, Graham of Inchbraikie, came by and tried to put an end to the proceedings. (This was despite his being one of the original complainants against her!) His protests, however, were in vain – the representatives of the kirk (and probably the gathered crowds as well) insisted the burning went ahead. Kate had noticed Inchbraikie's attempts, though, and just as the fire caught she bit a blue bead from her necklace and spat it at him shouting that as long as he and his family kept it his house would flourish. The flames soon consumed the unfortunate woman. The blue bead she spat at Inchbraikie became a valued heirloom and the family prospered through the years. The story was repeated time and again, for thousands of folk had come from miles around to see the end of Kate McNiven.

Kate McNiven

North Berwick Witches

One of the most striking landmarks in the Firth of Forth is the conically-shaped North Berwick Law. As I have already noted, the term 'law' often suggests a sacred site and it seems likely that North Berwick Law was suitable for the great seasonal fire festivals of Beltane and Samhain. It was here that one of the most famous witch covens in Scottish history used to meet.

In 1590, according to contemporary records, a local coven met with black work to do. A plot had been hatched by the Earl of Bothwell to murder his cousin, King James VI, and take over the throne. He was widely believed to have been initiated into the Devil's service and called upon the North Berwick coven to help implement his desires. One dark night in the port of Leith the witches gathered for a strange ceremony. They took a cat and tied gobbets of a hanged man's flesh to its paws. Incantations were muttered and then suddenly the screeching animal was flung into the seething waters of the Forth. A squall arose and a boat did founder, but it was the wrong boat. The intended victim of this bizarre ceremony was the king sailing back from Denmark with his new bride, Anne. The weather did worsen but the royal ship reached port safely.

The plot came to light when a local bailiff in Tranent, one David Seaton, began to suspect his servant Gillies Duncan was up to no good. When questioned she said nothing, but in those evil times suspicion of witchcraft was excuse enough to instigate extreme physical brutality with the avowed intention of extracting a confession. After various sadistic actions were carried out against her, including the mangling of her hands with pilnie-winks, or thumbscrews, she cracked and began to pour out a garbled series of confessions. According to her she was part of a coven that included a young local schoolmaster, John Fian, the aristocrat Euphemia MacLean, a midwife called Agnes Sampson and a local housewife, Barbara Napier. Sampson in particular was locally well known for her herbal cures and simples. When Fian was subjected to the grisly ritual of the boot, in which the victim's feet were slowly mangled, he confessed to devil worship but later retracted his confession. Despite further torture he remained steadfast but was eventually strangled

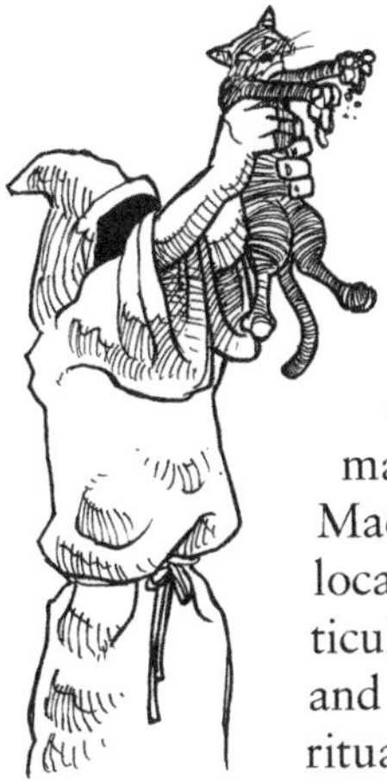

North Berwick witches

and burned on Edinburgh's Castle Hill. Sampson detailed various plots against the king including trying to get a piece of his personal clothing which she intended smearing with toad's venom. This she said would have caused him to die in torment. Tales were told of Sabbats attended by the Devil and the use of a *corp creagh*, or clay figure, representing the king. Napier said seven score witches were involved, while her co-accused Sampson claimed even more – 200. They described various rituals including a ring dance (once a standard at Beltane and other feasts) and a black mass. The king himself attended the trial and eventually interjected, calling all of the witches liars and effectively saying it was all fantasy.

Then came the strangest event of all. Agnes Sampson asked if she could speak to the king and tell him something only he could know. Moving off to the side, the midwife whispered something in the king's ear – the words that he had said to his new queen on their wedding night in Oslo when they were alone. This proof of supernatural powers was enough for the king and Sampson and Euphemia MacLean were executed soon after. Why Sampson should want to condemn herself by convincing the king of her supernatural powers is unclear but it is more than likely she was somewhat confused, having been tortured and interrogated for a considerable time. But she did convince the king. The rest of the confessions are full of the regularly recurring ideas that crop up throughout the period – and probably correspond much more closely to the fantasies of the ministers and other interrogators than to any actual rites and activities on the part of the women.

Boswell, said to have been the originator of the foul plot, has been suggested as the 'Devil' who led the activities at the various gatherings. He fled the country, dying in Italy 30 years later supposedly having carried on his necromantic activities there.

The king became even more interested in witchcraft and in fact went on to write a book on it himself called *Dæmonologie*. It is likely that it was this ongoing interest which inspired William Shakespeare to include the witch scene in Macbeth, performed before the king, who was by then also James I of England. To this day that is probably the most famous representation of Scottish witches and one which has set the pattern for so many others since.

The Witches of Auldearn

Just inland from the Moray coast and a few kilometres east of Nairn is Loch Loy (B18). It was here on a small farm that one of Scotland's most famous witches was raised. This was Isobel Goudie, one of the coven of witches who regularly met at the Auld Kirk of Auldearn (B67), built on the site of an earlier pagan sanctuary. This young woman was described as being very attractive with flaming red hair and mysterious dark eyes. It seems she met with a scholar of some sort in the nearby ruined Castle of Inshoch between Loch Loy (B18) and Auldearn and it was he who initiated her into the practice of witchcraft. Then she was baptised into the cult in the kirk of Auldearn itself. Later it is told that she went into the Downie Hills and met and drank with the Queen of the Fairies. She described the Devil manufacturing elf-arrow heads with his bare hands and handing over gold that turned to horse-dung within a day. She herself was shown how to make the *corp creagh*, or wax dummy, how to manufacture moon-paste and how to use fairy arrows. Here she also met notable people including Robert Gordon of Gordonstoun who was a privy councillor of Charles I. He was believed to have studied the black arts in Padua and Salamanca and was at last taken by the Devil near Birnie Kirk close to Elgin.

Isobel rose to some prominence in the cult but ultimately wearied of the life, gave herself up and confessed. She was tried in the very church in which she had been baptised as a witch – Auldearn – and was sentenced to be strangled and burned.

The link to the far past here is more than just the use of a sacred site. The elf-arrows Isobel Goudie talked of were long believed to be missiles from the 'little people' which were used to injure cattle or even humans. What they were is Stone Age flint arrowheads, often of remarkable workmanship. Coming across these in ploughed fields or on hillsides, people were impressed and it is little wonder that in those days before archaeology people saw such beautiful artefacts as magical rather than just remnants from the far distant past.

The Witch of Laggan

Just north of Kingussie (B35) at the very foot of the Monadhliath Mountains there was a green mound at Laggan (B37) where a witch used to dwell. She was often known to roam through the hills above Kingussie whatever the weather, going about her evil business. One day a hunter from nearby Gaick (B39) found himself caught in a vicious storm and took shelter in a rough bothy high in the hills. With him he had two hunting hounds which were his pride and joy. He had got a fire roaring and was sitting warming himself when he heard a mewling at the door. When he opened the door, there was a bedraggled black cat. The cat said she was in fact a poor witch in need of shelter and that she deeply regretted her misdeeds and wanted to repent, if only he would let her in by the fire. The two hounds growled deep in their throats and it was clear if the cat came in they might go for it. Despite his hatred of witchcraft, the hunter felt sorry for the creature and when she suggested he tie his hounds to the rantree of the bothy with a long hair she offered him, he said he would. However, he was a man of canny disposition and shushing his well-trained dogs, he only pretended to tie them up as he fastened the hair from the rantree to another spar in the roof.

The cat then came into the fire and at once began to swell in size. Suddenly she changed into human form and the hunter recognised the notorious witch, the 'good wife of Laggan'. She let out a cackle and said that now she had him. She called out 'Fasten, hair, fasten!' The magic hair at once contracted but all that happened was that the spar in the roof broke. The two hounds fell on the witch and began rolling about the floor with her. They were eventually thrown off, leaving their teeth in the hide of the foul creature. At once the witch changed shape again, this time into a raven. She flew out of the bothy door. The two hounds had been poisoned by biting the witch and the hunter could do nothing but watch them die. He buried the faithful beasts and then, as the storm had eased a bit he returned to Gaick. Getting home he was told that the 'good wife of Laggan' had caught a chill carrying peats and lay at death's door. At once he ran to Laggan and burst into the witch's house where in front of her neighbours he pulled the bedclothes off the old hag and showed the marks of his hounds' teeth in her skin. She had been sorely wounded by the hounds and began to cry in terror for she knew that when she died, her black master, Satan himself, would come to carry her off to Hell. With a final shriek of terror the old witch died in front of the astonished gathering.

Later that night two travellers were crossing the Monadhliath mountains on their way to Speyside when they saw a terrible apparition. A screaming blood-spattered woman was fleeing across the moor towards the kirkyard of Dalarossie (B38) closely pursued by two great black hounds and a black-clad horseman. They stopped and as the horseman passed them he jocularly asked if they thought the hounds would be able to catch up on their prey before she reached the kirkyard. With a terrifying laugh he then spurred his horse and went haring off after the woman and the hounds. The men got out as fast as they could but as they came down through the woods above Kingussie the black horseman passed them again. Over his saddle bow was the woman, the hounds still clinging to her. It seems the Evil One had had his sport and taken the soul of the Witch of Laggan.

Sometimes historical figures become the focus of stories of the supernatural. It as if the stories themselves have a life that sometimes must be renewed so they can fulfil their function. While most of these are female, folklore also records a few notable warlocks.

Michael Scot

Michael Scot was a twelfth-century mathematician and astrologer who had a reputation as a wizard throughout Europe. He travelled widely through the courts of Europe and owned a magic book which was buried with him in Melrose Abbey.

A tale is told of him catching and cooking a great white serpent near Drummochter (D1), the high pass through the Highlands south of Newtonmore (B36). It was said that the cooking of this beast gave him magic powers, as in the stories about Finn MacCool and the magic salmon or the Welsh Taliesin and the Cauldron of Cerridwen, where the heroes attain special powers by sucking on

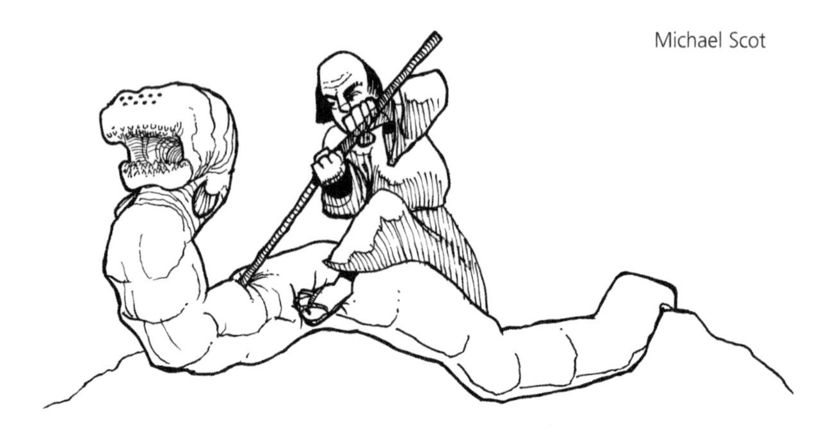
Michael Scot

their fingers burned by the cooking food. Like Thomas the Rhymer in later centuries, Scot's name became a byword all across Scotland although it was for magic and witchcraft rather than knowledge and wisdom.

The Wizard Laird of Skene

About ten kilometres to the west of Aberdeen is the House of Skene. In the late seventeenth century Alexander Laird of Skene was thought to be one of the foremost practitioners of 'the black art'. It is said that even on the brightest day he never cast a shadow. Like Michael Scot so many years before, he travelled Europe and indulged in all sorts of necromantic practices. In Italy he barely escaped with his life when the Devil came to claim his due from a group of necromancers. Skene escaped by telling him that there was yet another man behind him – so the Devil stole his shadow. This was not the only time he kept out of Auld Clootie's clutches.

The Wizard Laird was never seen without his familiars: a crow, a hawk, a magpie and a jackdaw. They were regularly seen with their master as he travelled in a coach drawn by coal-black horses with no visible harness, often on their way to the local kirkyard. Here he was said to open up graves and lift out the bodies of unbaptised infants as food for his familiars. Often this grisly crew would wander the hills and glens of the area searching for particular herbs to be used in potions and spells. Some of these he used to dispose of witches in the surrounding district for he was a man who would brook no competition. He was a terror to the whole district.

One Hogmanay night he was late getting home and decided to use his magic coach to cross Loch Skene (B48). That cold night the loch was covered by a thin film of ice which would clearly not support any normal coach. He told his birds that he would cross the loch safely as long as they did not doubt him. Then he told his coachman to press straight ahead with the horses at a gallop and no matter what not to look back. He was told to keep his eyes straight ahead on the Hill of Fare. The coach flew out over the ice with the four birds flying close to the horses' heads. But despite his warning the coachman felt himself being forced to turn around. No matter how hard he tried, it seemed irresistible to look over his shoulder. When he did his heart leaped in his mouth. There, beside his smiling master was the Deil himself.

Behind the coach galloped two great black hounds. Just at that point the ice split behind the coach and the hounds fell into the water. The horses galloped even faster and within minutes the terrified horseman was at the door of Skene Castle. Turning to look behind him, terrified of what he would see, he was amazed to see the Laird sitting there smiling as if nothing had happened.

An Edinburgh Warlock

The persecution of witches was widespread and long-lived and it was not always women who were the targets of the hysterical public reaction. In the middle of the seventeenth century one of Edinburgh's more notable citizens was Major Thomas Weir, commander of the City Guard and a noted Presbyterian.

He never married and his housekeeper was his spinster sister, Grizel. They appeared to be the absolute model of respectability except inasmuch as Grizel was subject to fits of extreme melancholia. Weir always did his best to help her in these situations and he was also known to be ready to pray beside the bed of anyone suffering from extreme illness or infirmity. It gradually became the subject of gossip that his capacity to pray seemed to be increased when he had his walking stick with him and that without it he hardly seemed the same man. This stick was oddly shaped and considered very unusual. Suspicions grew and Major Weir was called before the city magistrates to be interviewed. At once he confessed to a series of crimes and profligacies which shocked the city to the core. These crimes involved all sorts of wickedness and hypocrisy including incest with his sister. When she was questioned she admitted that she had been in communication with the Queen of the Fairies and not only confirmed her brother's confession but expanded on it. She claimed they could fly considerable distances and that they received all sorts of information about far-off events by magical means. The confessions could only have one outcome and they were both condemned to be strangled and then burned – which was considered a humanitarian option at the time.

The Major died first and went to his maker with a surly and impenitent air while Grizel had to be restrained from flinging off her clothes, an attempt that merely brought forward her strangulation. The Major's notorious stick was also burned and was said to have taken a long time to burn, twisting violently in the flames.

Most modern commentators are of the opinion that both the major and his sister were in fact probably suffering from some kind of delusional insanity but in those dangerous times when suspicion could be enough to bring death by burning, confessions were a guarantee of execution.

These types of confessions were obviously the result of torture and driven by deep-seated but ludicrous beliefs on the part of the inquisitors.

CHAPTER 8

Picts

BACK IN THE SEVENTEETH and eighteenth centuries 'Pictish' was used as a kind of general term to refer to Scottish ancestors. Constructions as far apart as Stone Age barrows and medieval deer dykes were all called Pictish. Today, some still think that anything old is Pictish, but scholars tend to put the 'Pictish Period' between 80 and 850 AD. 80 AD was the date of the battle of Mons Graupius when the Romans battled the Caledonians, later called Picts. Only the Romans have left us a record of this battle and argument still rages as to where it was fought. Not surprisingly, the Roman victory is reported as being total. The fact that the Romans retreated from Scotland north of the Forth soon after and only ever came back on temporary raids suggests a different interpretation, however.

In the middle of the ninth century the Picts amalgamated with the Scots of Dalriada – they had had several joint monarchs before this – and the country became known in time as Scotland. The Pictish language, which may have been something like Welsh, disappeared and this has led many people to speculate on the disappearance of the Picts themselves. While this has added to their mystique, the Picts are no less our ancestors than the Gaels, the Norse or the Angles.

Legends concerning the Picts are many. In one story from Fife, the Pechs (or Peghts, as they were generally called in the oral tradition) were wee short folk with red hair, long arms, broad feet and tremendous strength. They were the builders of all the old castles and forts in the land and would stand in a line from the quarry to the building site passing the stones from hand to hand until the building was finished. One version of the story says their feet were so broad that when it rained they could stand on their hands and use their feet as umbrellas!

Although the Picts left few written records and their domestic and military architecture blends in with that of other tribal peoples of Scotland, they have left one unique set of artefacts. These are the Pictish symbol stones, scattered from Fife to Farr in Sutherland and from the Western Isles to Buchan, and beyond into the Northern Isles. These beautiful stones, whose art may have influenced such works as the Books of Kells and Durrow, feature life-like animals and intricate geometric shapes that tell of a great artistic tradition. The symbol stones have become the subject of legend as much as have the Picts themselves.

The Maiden Stone

Nestled in the shade of Bennachie (B44) in Aberdeenshire is the Maiden Stone (B43). This magnificent granite stone is fading under the onslaught of twentieth-century pollution, but the symbols can still be discerned. And its story is still vivid.

There was a young lass called the Maid of Drumdorno who was known far and wide for her beauty. She had been wooed by many local lads and had at last agreed to marry one of her suitors. The afternoon before the wedding she was alone in the farmhouse baking bannocks and cakes for the following day and all the while day-dreaming about her wedding. Suddenly she became aware that she was being watched. She looked up and there at the open window was a tall, dark and good-looking stranger. She gave a little cry. The stranger spoke and told her she was doing her work well and looked good with it but maybe she was just a bit slow. She retorted that she was as quick as anyone else but, flattered by the attentions of the handsome stranger, exchanged a few words with him. She was quite clear about letting him know she was getting married the next day. He just laughed and said that was all very well but she would have to be a bit quicker at the baking to make a good wife. She took objection to this and told him so. Again he laughed and said he bet that he could build a road to the very top of Bennachie before she could finish her baking. He added that if she took the bet and he won, she would have to marry him instead of her intended. This was such a silly bet that she jokingly agreed and told the stranger to be on his way. Tipping his hat to her with a smile, he moved off.

She returned to her labours and soon all thought of the stranger had flown from her head. But a few hours later, just as the daylight was beginning to fade and the last batch of bannocks was ready to bake, she looked out the window. There in the fading light she could clearly see a brand new road leading all the way to the very top of Bennachie. She gasped and at that moment the stranger came into view. She now realised that she had entered a pact with the Devil. Panicking, she ran from the farm towards the Pittodrie woods. No one was about. She struggled to say a prayer but no words would come. The footsteps got louder and still she could not say the Lord's name. Just as the fiend caught up with her and grasped her waist, the prayer she had been unable to utter was answered, after a fashion. Instead of clutching a warm and vibrant lass the Devil was holding a piece of stone. He had been thwarted in his desires at the very last minute.

Although the lass had lost her life by being turned into stone she had been spared the fires of Hell and a great deal more besides. The abstract symbols on the stone – which has a small piece missing at the side of it where the Devil held on too hard – were said to represent the baking implements of the Maid of Drumdorno.

This tale ties together a Pictish symbol stone with the earlier causeway on Bennachie and was probably inspired by an attempt to decipher the meanings of the Pictish carvings.

Martin's Stane

Another Pictish symbol stone whose carvings might have inspired a local story is Martin's Stane (D15) on the back road from Dundee to the village of Tealing. Like many other such stones it has a serpent and 'Z-rod' carved on it as well as a mounted figure and a Pictish beast. These truly enigmatic figures look a little like a dolphin and are frequently seen on the symbol stones. The local tale has survived in a short poem which tells of a great dragon.

Martin's Stane

It was tempit at Pittempton,
Draggelt at Badragon,
Stricken at Strikemartin,
An killt at Martin's Stane.

There was once a farmer who lived at Pittempton (D16), on the northern edge of Dundee. Now the farmer at Pittempton had been blessed by having nine daughters, all of whom he loved dearly. The eldest had recently become betrothed to a local man called Martin. One hot summer's day the farmer was working hard in his fields. He grew thirsty and called for his eldest daughter to go to the well and fetch him a drink of water. Off she went and when after a few minutes there was no sign of her coming with the water, he sent his next eldest daughter to hurry her up. When the second daughter also did not return, he called for his third eldest daughter to go and see what was happening. And again she did not return. So one by one the farmer sent his lovely daughters to the well. When even the youngest had not returned he was sure they were playing a trick on him and went to the well himself.

There he saw a terrible sight. Round the well lay a great, coiled, dragon-like serpent. Scattered about were the limbs of his nine daughters. The beast had killed them all. He let out a great shriek and ran to summon his neighbours. Several had heard his cries and in minutes a large crowd of men and women carrying various farm implements as weapons descended on the well. Seeing them coming the dragon shot off towards the north hotly pursued by Martin who had picked up a large club. As the great scaly creature got to the Dighty Burn, Martin caught up with it and raised his club. The pursuing crowd yelled out as one, 'Strike, Martin!' and he gave the beast a crashing blow. This only served to make it double its speed and it soon outstripped him. Help was at hand, however, for horses had been brought and soon Martin and several others were in hot pursuit of the monster. They quickly had it surrounded and after a short struggle killed and buried the fearsome beast. It is on this spot that tradition tells that Martin's Stane was raised and the village of Strathmartin itself, close to Pittempton, is said to have once been called Strikemartin.

A Pictish Centre?

Other Pictish stones were once to be found in this area, one with a carving of a man with a large club over his shoulder. Others, of which one is in nearby Dundee Museum, all had serpents of different kinds on them. This suggests some sort of important Pictish centre here, perhaps a temple of some sort. What is certain, however, is that this is not the only story of the nine maidens. The hills to the north of the stone have a different nine maidens who were known as Pictish saints, and other tales tell of similar events in Aberdeenshire where there are Nine Maidens wells in many locations. There are also links to King Arthur and the nine maidens of Avalon, Apollo and the nine muses and the Norse god Heimdall who had nine mothers. Perhaps what we have here is a remnant of a memory of groups of pagan priestesses. Whatever the Nine Maidens were, their hold on the public imagination lasted a long time.

Sueno's Stone

There is a strong connection with Scandinavia in the story of Sueno's Stone. Though the stone itself was found buried in the eighteenth century, the tale carries us back to the Dark Ages. We are told that the stone commemorates a battle between the local people and an invading force of Norsemen. Fighting had been going on for many years as the Norsemen had started to settle in the area. In the struggle for overall control of Moray the principal antagonists were Maelbrigde, the Mormaer of Moray and the Norse Jarl Sigurd. (Mormaer and Jarl are terms meaning something close to 'high chief'.) They agreed to settle matters once and for all by a battle where each would bring forty horsemen. On the chosen day Maelbrigde, known as 'the Buck-toothed' because of a peculiarly long eyetooth he had like an animal's fang, set off for the battlefield with his men. As they approached the selected spot they saw the forty Norse horses ahead. However, each of the Norsemen's horses carried two warriors – Maelbrigde had been tricked. With such an advantage the Norsemen were assured of victory and the men of Moray were all killed. In celebration of this victory the Norse beheaded their enemies and returned to their camp, each astride a horse. Sigurd, in emulation perhaps of ancient tribal tradition, had taken Maelbrigde's head with him and slung it from the pommel of his saddle. As they rode, singing of their triumph, and no doubt drinking in celebration, Maelbrigde's bucktooth began rubbing on Sigurd's thigh, eventually piercing the skin. Although superficially just a scratch, the wound festered and within three days Sigurd died in agony from blood-poisoning. Maelbrigde had his revenge.

Vanora's Stone

Another Pictish symbol stone with a remarkable story can be found in the wonderful little museum of Pictish symbol stones in the Strathmore village of Meigle (D14), 20 kilometres north-west of Perth. Among this collection is the great cross-slab known to locals as Vanora's Stone. Vanora's Stone is unusual in that it once formed part of a complex linked monument of different stones although we have no clear idea of how it used to look. On the side opposite the magnificent cross there is a scene

Vanora's Stone

which has been interpreted by various learned commentators as representing Daniel in the lion's den. It shows a gowned figure flanked by four-legged animals with heavy shoulders or manes. (Many Pictish symbol stones show both biblical and pagan iconography and in pre-literate societies it is feasible that older stories could be attached to biblical symbolism.)

The legend of Vanora's Stone involves King Arthur. There are many places in Scotland that bear the name of Arthur – Arthur's Seat in Edinburgh, Ben Arthur (C14) in Cowal, another Arthur's Seat (D11) further up Strathmore from Meigle, and a handful of them are scattered in the landscape around Meigle. The mythical Arthur was almost certainly common amongst the traditions of all the P-Celtic-speaking tribal peoples of Britain (whose languages survive as Welsh, Cornish and Breton). The idea of Arthur belonging as much to Pictish Scotland as to Wales or Cornwall is not really strange at all, even though the Pictish language itself died out over a thousand years ago.

Vanora was the wife of the great king, Arthur. Having defeated his enemies, Arthur decided to go on a pilgrimage to Rome, leaving his nephew Mordred as regent. Hardly had he set out when Vanora became involved with Mordred and they began to rule the land together. Whether Vanora was seduced by Mordred or the other way around is unclear but they soon ruled as man and wife with the support of Mordred's own Pictish troops. Arthur was still in Britain when he heard the news and immediately headed north to raise his followers and remove the usurpers. The battle where Mordred and Arthur are said to have met was at Camlaan, on the Forth. Mordred was defeated and killed, but Arthur was also fatally wounded and soon passed away. Vanora was imprisoned in the great Iron Age fort on nearby Barry Hill (D20) while her fate was decided. She was guilty of adultery but had betrayed the king and, therefore, his people. Such was the blackness of her deeds, the story goes, that the wisemen and priests who considered her fate decided she should be made to suffer as dishonourable a death as possible. So it was decreed she should be ripped apart by a pack of wild dogs. The sentence was duly carried out. And this is the how the locals interpreted the scene on the cross-slab.

Following her execution, her body was buried as oaths and imprecations were heaped upon her burial in a manner very suggestive of ancient pagan practice. This burial is said to be in Vanora's Mound in the kirkyard of Meigle and it was believed until recently that any young woman foolish enough to stand upon the mound would be made barren – such was the power of the curses heaped upon it so long ago. This was clearly not known to a local photographer who until quite recently had the habit of posing happy newlyweds on the mound!

Norrie's Law

A mile or so north of Largo Law (D51) on the north side of the Forth is a hill said to have received its cleft shape from a ploughshare thrown by the Devil. In the same place on the farm of Auchendowie there used to be a tumulus, or burial mound. The site of the mound is still marked on maps though little now remains of what was known locally as Norrie's Law (D49). On the slopes of Largo Law itself until a generation or two back children would play a widely-known game with a particular local variant. One child would stand in front of a group of pals and say,

'A'll tell ye a story aboot Tammie o Norrie if ye dinnae speak in the middle o it. Will ye no?'

The intention is to make one of the other, probably younger children say no and thus prevent the story from being told. The difference from most versions of this bairns' game is the mention of Tammie o Norrie, an unfortunate local cowherd.

It was told that a ghost haunted the slopes of Largo Law, condemned to roam the earth until he could unburden himself of the secret he had died to save: the location of buried gold on Largo Law. A local shepherd on Balmain (D50) farm became obsessed with the idea of this gold and decided that he would approach the ghost and relieve it of its burden. It took all his courage but one evening he went to Largo Law as night fell, hoping to meet the unfortunate spirit. He soon spotted the ethereal figure and approached it, asking what was keeping it from its rest. The spectre looked long at him and the shepherd's blood ran cold. Then the spirit spoke:

If Auchendowrie cock disnae craw
An the herd o Balmain disnae blaw,
A'll tell ye where the gowd is on Largo Law.

This was to have been at eight o'clock the following evening. The shepherd, excited at the notion of impending riches, did his best to ensure the ghost's conditions would be met. That night the rooster of Auchendowrie farm mysteriously disappeared. The shepherd went the following morning to speak to the cowherd of Balmain, Tammie o Norrie. After trying to wheedle him into not blowing his horn to summon the cattle into the byre that evening, he finally threatened to kill him if he dared do so. Sure that he had frightened Tammie sufficiently, the shepherd made his way to Largo Law as eight o'clock approached. Just as the wraith appeared and was about to speak, the sound of a cow horn floated through the air from Balmain. The ghost, deprived of its release from earthly torment, spat forth the words

Woe tae the man that blew that horn,
Fae oot o that spot he shall neer be borne

... and disappeared.

In a blind rage the shepherd ran north, the thought of killing the Balmain cowherd pulsing in his mind. When he got to what is now the site of Norrie's Law he was too late. There stood the figure of Tammie o Norrie, horn at his lips, having been turned to stone. The local people tried to shift the unfortunate man, but a magical force prevented them. Instead, they heaped a great mound of earth over the cowherd and this was given the name of Norrie's Law.

This story seems to be a degenerate version of an even older tale. In this rendition, the mound contains the body of a warrior called Norroway who was buried astride his horse in a suit of silver armour. What we do know is that in the 1830s a local cadger, or carter, was digging sand out of the hill when he made a remarkable discovery of silver. Over a few years he sold most of it to a silversmith in Cupar (D47) who melted it down and re-used it. Eventually the cadger's conscience got the better of him and he handed over the few remnants he had to the widow of the local landowner, the recently deceased General Durham. She in turn donated the material to the then Museum of Antiquities and the few magnificent remnants of the original Norrie's Law hoard can be seen in the new Museum of Scotland. These are a few bits and pieces including a pair of pins with Pictish symbols, a couple of lozenge-shaped items that might once have been part of a corselet of mail, and pieces of a sword hilt, helmet and scabbard.

The Sleeping Pict

Robert Louis Stevenson wrote about the Picts in his poem 'The King of the Picts', but his father had a closer connection to that ancient people. He was in Orkney surveying a site for a new lighthouse when he and a colleague were visited in their lodgings by a distraught local. He begged them to come with him and help him and his neighbours with a desperate problem. Their help was sought because they were educated men and whatever the problem was it was clearly taxing the powers of the local community.

He told them that a Pict had turned up in their village. This was met with utter disbelief by Stevenson and his friend but the local was insistent. He described a wee dark, hairy man with great big feet, clad in strangely shaped shoes, dressed in rags and without speech. He had come into the village and collapsed. The engineers were hardly keen to go outside – it was a wild night and they were comfortable by the fire. However the man was in such a state of distress that they thought they should try and help. At last they agreed to go.

When they reached the nearby village they were ushered into a humble cottage, surrounded by a crowd, even in the biting cold. Inside, yet more people were grouped around a bed on which lay the Pict. The mood of the people was sombre, and mutterings of 'Get rid of it' could be heard. In truth, the man asleep on the bed was very small, not much over four feet, and had a mass of unkempt hair and a big black beard. His clothes were made of rags stitched together and his feet were encased in extremely crude boots, obviously hand-made by someone with little if any cobbling skill.

Stevenson recognised the sleeping Pict. He was a man who had been a shopkeeper in Edinburgh until one day he got the call to go on the road and spread the word of the Lord. He gave away all his worldly goods and left the city to wander wherever his feet took him, spreading the Gospel and living as simply as he could. He had eventually ended up in Orkney, got lost, and by the time he found the village he was in a state of absolute exhaustion, made worse by not having eaten for several days, if not longer. His life on the road accounted for his appearance and he had naturally made his own boots, with no skill or instruction in that particular art. The villagers took some convincing but when the Pict at last opened his eyes, recognised Stevenson and spoke to him in Scots, their scepticism disappeared. They feared no more that an ancient Pict had burst forth from a burial mound to wreak havoc among them.

CHAPTER 9

Giant Lore

ALL OVER SCOTLAND SCRAPS of ancient mythology survive about giants. In Cromarty it is said that two vast boulders lying on the beach near Edderton (B9) were flung from the Hill of Struie, locally called Gilltrax. A variant of the same story concerns the Goors of Gowrie (D19), flung by the Devil from St Andrew's (D48) to Invergowrie, just west of Dundee. Another tale tells of a Deil's Stane flung by the giant on Norman's Law (D46) at the giant who resided on Dundee Law. In fact such tales are commonly used to explain the rocky slopes of many Scottish and Irish hills and mountains. Another famous giant lived on the hill of Bennachie (B44) in Aberdeenshire, famous in story and song and the site of many ancient monuments. An ancient ballad tells us the story.

Lang Johnnie Moir

Lang Johnnie Moir hailed from Rhynie, the village at the foot of Bennachie. At 20 years of age he was over four metres tall and was a full two metres across the shoulder. Even Johnnie's sword was three metres long. He was of an adventurous disposition and one day he headed off to London without letting anyone know. A giant like him was sure to catch the eye and he was not long in the English capital when a bonnie young lass fell in love with him. The feeling was entirely mutual but there was a problem. The lass Johnnie had fallen for was none other than the King of England's daughter. When the king heard of what was happening he locked the young lass up in a tower and left her there to starve. He would not hear of a daughter of his going to marry a Scottish commoner, even if he was a giant. There and then he sent out men to apprehend the young giant whom he intended to hang from a tall, tall tree. On hearing this Johnnie said the king was welcome to try and

Lang Johnnie Moir

capture him. However, kings are never loath to use cunning instead of courage and men were dispatched to spike Johnnie's nightly gallon of ale.

When Johnnie awoke he found himself bound in thick iron bands and chains. Luckily, he had made friends with a wee lad who worked in his lodgings and the young lad agreed to go all the way to Rhynie for help. Off went the lad over brae and burn, by hill and river. Arriving in Rhynie he went immediately to the tallest giant he could find there. This was Auld Johnnie, the young giant's uncle, and the wee lad told him to get to London quick and to bring Jock o Noth with him. Jock o Noth was the giant who lived on the Tap o Noth (B40) another dominating hill some 20 kilometres west of Bennachie. Auld Johnnie ran up to Mither Tap on Bennachie and called out to Jock o Noth to come and help rescue young Johnnie. Even that distance away Jock heard the call and in no time at all the two great giants were on their way south to London. What a sight they made as they hurried south, looming above the trees, their brows a metre across and their shoulders near three metres broad.

When they got to London they found the gates of the City locked and barred against them and from inside they could hear the sound of a slow drum beat and the ringing of church bells.

Auld Johnnie hammered on the gate and demanded to know

what was going on from the gatekeeper who looked out of a window at the knocking. The gatekeeper said it was nothing much, they were just about to hang a great big Scot called Lang Johnnie Moir.

At this the giants demanded entry and finally kicked a great hole in the city walls and clambered through. They hastened to the town hall and there they saw the young giant on the gibbet tree, a noose around his neck.

Before anything else was done the great giant asked his nephew what he had been charged with that these Londoners meant to hang him. When they heard that the sentence was for falling in love, the two giants were furious and their rage grew even more when they heard how Johnnie had been captured. Drawing their swords, they demanded that the shackles and bands be removed and Johnnie be returned his good broadsword. Despite being brave and battle-hardened men, the King's guard had no intention of trying to fight with these gigantic warriors, now brandishing their massive broadswords over their heads. Johnnie was released.

They wasted no time heading directly to the king's palace, demanding to see his daughter. The terrified king sent for his daughter to be released and brought to the palace. Then a priest was summoned and the young couple were wed. The giants spurned the offer of a dower from the king – they were all as rich as they needed to be with castles and farms, plenty of men to work the land, flocks and herd beyond number and countless chests brimming with gold. Then there was one of the finest wedding celebrations ever seen in old London town, lasting all of seven days and seven nights, although the king did not appear to enjoy it much. Then the newly-weds headed back to Bennachie with the two old giants and the wee lad who had carried the message.

The Fianna

Scotland has many tales of Finn MacCool and the Fianna, or Fenians, a legendary warrior-band whose origins are in early Irish literature. In later tradition, they are known as a race of ancient giants, stories of which entranced generations of Gaelic speakers at céilidhs through much of Scotland. The Fianna's presence is marked in placenames and legends throughout the country. The basis for the stories seems to have been a practice in ancient Irish and Scottish tribal society where young men would gather together in bands during the summer to learn and practice military skills and hunting. This was how individual lads became tribal warriors and these groups could also be used to defend the land against invaders and slave-raiders. In some cases they would even hire themselves out as mercenaries. And it kept the young men out from under the feet of everyone else.

The Sma Glen (D31) is an area rich in traditions of the Fianna. At Fendoch (D32), overlooking the A822 north of Crieff, there is said to have been a wooden palisaded fort inhabited in the distant past by the Fianna. They lived here with their wives, also of gigantic stature. One day Finn and his companions decided to go and hunt for wild boar in the mountains to the north. One of them had to stay behind to watch over the women, although it was common enough knowledge that the women were actually quite capable of looking after themselves. Lots were drawn and the task of staying with the women fell to Garaidh who, though he was a fine and experienced warrior, adept in both battle and the hunt, was vain. He was extremely proud of his long, golden hair which he wore in braids and was often to be seen combing and braiding. Most of the ancient tribal warriors of Scotland wore their hair long and had moustaches which necessitated a deal of care – but Garaidh was a bit of a poser.

After the warriors left for the hunt in the morning Garaidh, considerably put out at missing the fun, combed and braided his hair as the women went about their daily business. As the day wore on it got hotter and hotter and Garaidh eventually stretched himself on the ground outside the fort and fell asleep. The women, seeing him lying there with this long braids carefully spread on the ground around his head, decided to play a trick on him. A couple of them sneaked up on the sleeping warrior and proceeded to pin each of his braids securely in the ground with hammers and pegs. Then, retreating back inside the fort, closing and barring the gate, they gave a great shout. Garaidh leapt to his feet, drawing his sword and adopting a defensive posture all in the one movement.

His long glorious braids were torn from his head and blood was streaming from his torn scalp. He let out a great roar. The women were looking over the fort wall, pointing and laughing. Garaidh turned to see them and his pain turned to blind rage. He ran and hammered on the gate, but the fort was well-built and the gate stood firm. With the women laughing and jeering his anger and hurt pride could only grow. He ran off, the women hooting after him.

He was back in minutes with great bundles of dry straw and brushwood which he began to heap around the wooden fort. The women, realising his intention was to burn the fort, soon stopped laughing and began to tell him to stop. As he continued with his work their demands turned to pleas – after all it had only been a practical joke. Garaidh ignored them. When he had piled enough kindling round the fort, he set fire to it and stood back to watch it burn. It had been a long, dry summer and within seconds flames were licking up the walls of the fort and the palisades themselves soon burst into flame. The cries and the shrieks were horrible and Garaidh took his place in front of the gate sword in hand, ready to strike down any woman who dared try and escape. Soon the entire fort was blazing and the screams of the women died away.

Away in the hills to the northeast Finn and his men were following the trail of a fine boar when Finn himself turned and looked to the southwest. A great plume of smoke rose in the sky from Fendoch. At once he turned and began to run back, followed immediately by the well-trained Fianna. By the time they got to Fendoch there was nothing but a smoking heap of ashes and no sign of Garaidh or any of their wives. Once they saw Garaidh's braids, still pinned to the ground, they deduced what had happened. The grief-stricken Fianna soon set out on a grim hunt for Garaidh, who had fled the scene of the crime once his head had cleared and he realised what he had done. They found him in a cave further up Glen Almond and he was killed on the spot.

It is from this time on, we are told, that the end of the Fianna was in sight: there were no women left and there could be no more children of the Fianna. This is why we no longer have such magnificent giants in Scotland.

The Muileartach

Earlier we learned the extent of goddess tales in Scotland's landscape, most of these represented as giant females. One such was the Muileartach of Mull. The Muileartach is said to have walked out of the sea to approach Finn's dwelling. On the way, she pulled up a tree, swept off the branches and used it for a stick. She came to Finn's door and begged to be let in, claiming to be nothing but a poor old woman wanting to warm herself at the fire. Now Finn could understand everything by biting his thumb, which he burned on the Salmon of Knowledge when he was a child. So biting his thumb, he realised who was at the door and refused to open it. At this the Muilertach showed her true colours and kicked the door in, snatching Finn's famous Cup of Victory. This vessel was a magic cup which gave mysterious powers to Finn as well as being able to magically feed the Fianna. Two of the Fianna, Caoilte and Oscar chased her and regained the cup after a short fight.

Another story on Mull relates how one day the Muileartach was returning from a journey to the north. She had one foot on Mull and one on the Ardnamurchan peninsula, straddling the Sound of Mull (A20). In this awkward position a ship came sailing through the sound, causing her to lose her balance, fall into the water and drown. She must have been a real giant for the Sound of Mull is nearly two kilometres wide at its narrowest point, but what size must the ship have been to coup such a giantess?

The Making of the Outer Hebrides

An old tale tells us that long, long ago, before the clans had been formed or the druids had worshipped at stone circles and before even the Outer Hebrides were formed, a great giant lived in Stack Rock, far out in the Western Sea. This terrifying and enormous giant had nine heads and nine mouths, each with a fearsome appetite. His preferred dish was a young woman and he was in the habit of raiding Inner isles like Skye, Raasay, Rum (A27) and Eigg, stealing maidens, nine at a time. He would then take them back to his castle and each would be a meal for one of his nine mouths.

One day he had made a successful raid on Skye and was heading home through the ocean, unaware that one of his captives was promised in marriage to a young man of great character. Refusing to mourn for his stolen fiancée, the young hero went into the Cuillinns to ask help from a kelpie that lived in an isolated lochan. After some bargaining the kelpie agreed to help and the pair of them set off to Stack Rock. Though the fight was long and hard, they finally managed to cut off eight of the giant's great ugly heads. This weakened the monster enough for the hero to kill him with a thrust to the heart. He then released his intended and her companions, who were all very grateful for their rescue. Before returning to Skye they wondered what to do with the giant's body and eight heads. There was not sufficient ground on Stack Rock to bury him so pieces of the great cadaver were thrown into the sea, where they floated. The hero and the nine maidens all mounted on the broad back of the kelpie and headed back to Skye.

Well, the sea is great and proved capable of dealing with this monster. Birds began to descend in flocks upon the body of the giant just as shoals of fish swam to it under the waves. Soon the body of the vast monster was reduced to bones. Even these remains were too large simply to wear away and there they lay lashed by wind and rain, giving shelter to birds and fish until they merged with the flotsam and jetsam of the sea and vast fields of sea-wrack. The body formed itself into the cliffs and rocks of the long islands of Harris (A7) and Lewis (A5), North and South Uist (A10), Benbecula and Barra (A14). Even today you can see the outline of the giant in the shape of these isles, with the last head the Butt of Lewis (A1) and the soles of his feet forming the cliffs of South Bernera (A16). His eight heads became the islands of Bernera, Eriskay (A13), Mingulay (A15), Vallay, Gramsay, Taransay (A6), Pabbay (A8) and Killegray (A9), although they are of different sizes.

Guru

A tale of a giantess from Sutherland may be a remnant of Norse mythology. This part of Scotland was ruled by the King of

Norway until the sixteenth century and many Norse people settled in the seven hundred years before then.

Guru was a giantess who came to Sutherland from Norway with her husband when the old Norse gods fled before the coming of Christianity, around 1,000 AD. They set themselves up on an island in a loch not far from Forsinard (B5). Being giants from the pagan world they had no souls and thus there was no real place for them in Christendom. One day they heard that St Olaf had sent some missionaries to Sutherland to convert the local pagans. Soon they saw one coming out to their island in a boat. Without coming ashore, he told them that their home would provide the perfect location for the church he intended building and asked them to leave. They told him to be on his way. Guru's husband walked into the loch, lifted up the boat and threw it to the far shore with the priest still in it. The saint raised his cross in retaliation and turned the giant into a pillar of stone.

Guru

Guru was distraught and began weeping and crying about how good her man had been to her as well as to all the local humans. The priest, perhaps beginning to have second thoughts about his rash action, went off and consulted with the local populace. None had a bad word to say about the now petrified giant. So the priest then made a concession: the giant might come back to life for one night a year if embraced by one of his own kind who would be prepared to give up a hundred years of his or her own life to do so. The distraught Guru agreed to this deal and soon the priest left to convert pagans somewhere else. But he kept his word: every year at yuletide Guru and her husband were re-united.

Then one year a young couple landed on the island begging shelter. Guru said they could stay there on her island, as long as they went away each Yuletide and this they agreed to. A year or two later the young lass, named Astog, became pregnant; the baby was due in midwinter.

Astog's child was born on Christmas Eve. Guru could not bring herself to turn the young mother and the new-born child out. She made the lass and her husband promise not to look outside or mention the Holy Name at all on Christmas Day. But as the day wore on the child began to cry and the lass shushed her and blessed her unthinkingly. Guru's husband had been flesh until that moment but was now immediately turned back into stone – forever. Guru let out a heart-rending scream. With her husband gone for good she could not bear to live on the island any longer. She gave it to Astog and her husband on the condition they treated a local group of hill-dwarves with kindness. She went off to live out her life wandering the face of the earth.

A few years later St Olaf's priest returned to the district to find that paganism had reasserted itself. He wondered why his preaching of God's love had had so little success in the area.

Fear Liath Mor

Ben Macdui (B34) is Scotland's second highest mountain. It is the highest of the Cairngorms, the highest section of the Grampian Mountains, an area known for startling beauty and sudden life-threatening changes in weather patterns. Over the years many people have lost their lives in these mountains and many others have come close to death. Some of these have come across Fear Liath Mor, the Big Grey Man of Ben Macdui. As all who have tramped the mountain tops in mist can tell, the senses will shift, and even familiar features can take on strange and eerie aspects. Small rock faces can suddenly seem like vast walls, and cairns and scarps can loom out of the mist like great beasts crouching to spring. But there is more to Fear Liath Mor than this.

There are those who believe that he is a malevolent spirit on the lookout for lone climbers with the intention of driving them over Lurcher's Gully into the pass of Lairig Ghru (B33) far below. Several people have reported hearing footsteps following them as they crossed the plateau – one footstep to every three or four of their own – and there are numerous sightings of a vast grey

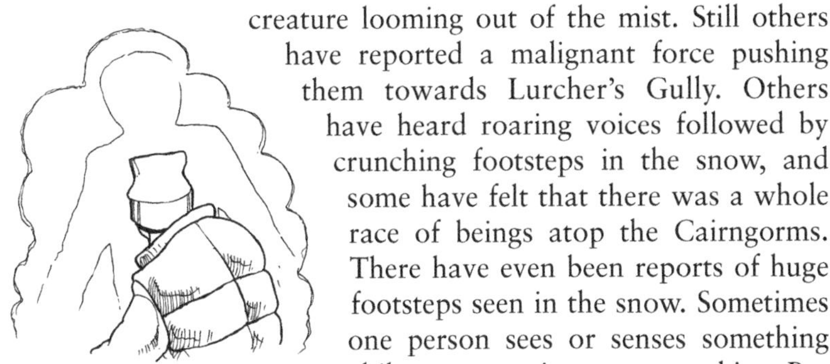
Fear Liath Mor

creature looming out of the mist. Still others have reported a malignant force pushing them towards Lurcher's Gully. Others have heard roaring voices followed by crunching footsteps in the snow, and some have felt that there was a whole race of beings atop the Cairngorms. There have even been reports of huge footsteps seen in the snow. Sometimes one person sees or senses something while a companion senses nothing. But all these events have happened in the mist when normal sense and hearing are considerably altered. Mist seems to bend the light, deaden sound and then amplify it as winds whirl and the moisture condenses or dissipates. There has also been a 'rational' explanation – the apparition is said to be a natural phenomenon, the Brocken Spectre. Named for a German mountain, this phenomenon is no more than one's own shadow greatly enlarged in the mist. Those who have walked the Scottish mountains in mist know, however, that life itself seems very different in the cold damp surroundings and the world seems no more than a few yards across. Local people in the straths and glens of Rothiemurchus simply accept that the Big Grey Man is up there.

The lore of these giants and the massive Fianna was an important part of the process of passing on understanding of the physical world and the necessary rules of society that had been handed down through the generations by word of mouth. As to whether giants actually existed, there have been reports of giant skeletons in the past and there might yet be surprises in store for us.

CHAPTER 10

Stone Circles and Standing Stones

ALL OVER SCOTLAND WE find standing stones. Sometimes one stands alone in a field. In other cases, we find a circle of stones in now out of the way locations. While we know that many of these erections were raised in the Stone Age, we have no definite idea of their use. The effort required to raise some of the larger stones illustrates their importance – not to mention their organising and transporting. Although we are learning that the lives of hunter-gatherers and early agriculturists were not as difficult and wearisome as they were once thought to be, it is clear they put hard work into erecting these stones.

Much romanticised speculation has been written over the years concerning druids, stone circles and standing stones. The druids, first of all, existed thousands of years after the stones were raised – and it is unlikely they formed an organised movement in any case. But these myth-based ideas on origin are interesting. One such comes from a man called Donovan, a diviner working and living in Dartmoor in southwest England. He said he dowsed the same sort of patterns below stone circles as he found at deer rutting sites. Donovan suggested that early people, seeing the deer return year after year to mate at the same sites, began to associate such locations with fertility and the ongoing turn of the seasons and raised their own sacred sites there.

Other scholars, like the late Alexander Thom, have concentrated on the mathematics and astronomical alignments of the circles, suggesting common units of measurement and a widespread awareness of astronomy at some level. The idea that our ancestors watched the stars turning in the heavens makes sense, and it is easy to believe that some of the circles were in some way arranged in relation to the position of the moon and particularly bright stars or planets. Recumbent stone circles with a flat horizontal stone in their southeast quadrants are unique to northeast Scotland and might have been associated with the moon.

In the Gaelic oral tradition many of these stones are known as *fir bhreige*, false men. The story is that a group of people, ignoring warnings from their priests, decided to play music and dance on the Sabbath. When they were in the height of revelry they were suddenly transformed into stone in punishment. This story was told of the great circle of Calanish (A4) in Lewis as well as many others and seems to have been an attempt to keep people away from the stones. The idea is common all over the United Kingdom. What we can say is that the stones themselves must have held a strong attraction for the Church to come up with this explanation of their creation.

Clach Ossian

It is possible, if unproveable, that some of the beliefs and practices associated with the ancient standing stones and circles stem from the time they were erected, roughly 3000 – 1000 BC. Belief in such sites is tenacious, remaining in place for thousands of years sometimes – as in the case of Clach Ossian, the Stone of Ossian. This massive great boulder lies just off the road in the Sma Glen, a few miles north of Crieff in Strathearn.

Clach Ossian

In the 1730s the London government was making a concerted attempt to open up the Highlands and change the way of life of the clanspeople, still living much as their Iron Age ancestors had two thousand years before. Although the clan system was breaking down in the face of the new money economy and increasing governmental centralization, people still held to the old beliefs. General Wade had been put in charge of driving highways along the old drove roads into the Highlands and one autumn in the mid-1730s his engineers, with accompanying military escort, were pushing the road through the Sma Glen. Right in the way of the new road there stood a massive boulder on a raised area. Using the technology of the day, levers and combined horse and manpower, the army engineers managed to move the stone off to the side. Then there was sudden consternation as it was realised there was a pit below where the stone had stood. And in the pit was an ancient urn. The officers in charge called an immediate halt to work and word was sent back to General Wade that they had found a Roman burial! The officers knew all about the Romans, fine models that they were for the expanding British Empire, but knew little or nothing of Scotland's past. A guard was set over the burial as work finished for the day and the soldiers and engineers went back down to Fendoch, itself the reputed site of a Fianna fort. The guard settled down for the night. A couple of hours later he noticed a procession of torches coming towards him from the south; the sound of bagpipes echoed through the glen. The eerie lights grew closer and well before the crowd reached the stone he had given up all thought of protecting the archaeological site, orders or not. The torches were carried by a substantial crowd of local people, amongst whom were the kilted soldiers from the Highland regiment. Many of these people were Gaelic speakers and although they might not have been able to read, they knew the great stories of Finn MacCool. These formed part of the great treasury of Gaelic lore which fired the European success of James McPherson at the end of the century. His Ossianic poems drew from the same well that was inspiring these people, for they knew who was buried under the great stone. For generations it had been told that this was the final resting place of Ossian himself, who had transformed the heroic deeds of Finn and the Fianna into poetry and song. Ossian had been Finn's son and was long believed to have outlived his fellow Fianna. The people had come to pay their respects – and more.

The urn was raised from the pit and carried reverently to the top of nearby Dunmore (D33), a piper playing. Here, within a hill-fort believed to have been occupied by the Fianna themselves, the ashes were ceremoniously laid to rest. The locals left, their work completed.

In all likelihood the urn and its ashes were much earlier than the time when tribes like the mythological Fianna may have lived – what little we know suggests a Stone Age origin. However the sanctity of the site itself and respect for whoever was buried there had clearly continued through linguistic and societal changes. The reverence of the people for their culture had led them to intervene directly in what they saw as a sacrilegious act and they had made sure their great hero was safe from further disturbance. To this day no one knows exactly where the ashes were reburied.

This type of linkage between Stone Age monuments and the heroic saga of the Fianna happened elsewhere, too. (In one sense, this is hardly surprising, since there is no evidence to show that the population of Scotland has ever been totally overrun by invaders.) The standing stones and circles were erected by the ancestors of the people who became the Highland and Lowland clans – and today's Scots.

The Stone of Odin

A totally different kind of belief was associated with another stone much further north, on Orkney. Here on the main island of Orkney (B3) a few miles north of Kirkwall, are the awesome Stones of Stenness (B2). This ruined stone circle once boasted twelve stones, of which four remain. The circle is 31.1 metres in circumference. Local belief was that this and its partner circle, the larger Ring of Brodgar (142 metres in diameter) were once the sites of sun and moon worship. One of the Stenness stones was particularly note-worthy. This was the Stone of Odin, a six-metre high, one-metre wide and 40-centimetre thick monolith destroyed in 1814, through which there was a hole. Through this hole, lovers would clasp their hands and enter into marriage. (This is a variant on the time-honoured custom of handfasting, a form of marriage by public declaration. Couples who wished to divorce could do so by leaving through separate doors of a church after the service.)

But Odin is none other than the chief god of the Norse pantheon. Norwegian culture was very important in Scotland and not until the sixteenth century did Norwegian kings give up their ownership of Orkney and Shetland. The Shetland dialect of Scots, called Norn, still holds many words and phrases of Norse origin.

The area around the Brodgar and Stenness stones is full of barrows and stone alignments and it is more than probable that the pagan Norsemen in Orkney were using the site much as it had been used millennia before they arrived. Nearby is the magnificent megalithic tomb of Maes Howe (B1) on which tradition is sadly silent. It was raided by Vikings at some point, who left runes carved on its walls.

Deil's Stanes

All over Scotland there are stories of supernatural beings throwing great boulders vast distances. When the Devil throws stones, he is often said to have been aiming at a saint or priest building a church. One of these is the Puddock Stone at Invergowrie (B19), just outside Dundee on the north bank of the River Tay. Tradition tells us that St Boniface was overseeing the building of a church when the devil became aware of him. At the time the devil was walking near St Andrews some twenty miles away. Angered at the saint's presumption, he picked up the stone and threw it at the church. He missed by quite a bit – the Puddock Stone landed half a mile to the north of the church! Also in the area, between the site of the church and Invergowrie Bay (now much reduced due to a policy of landfilling by Dundee City Council) there were the Goors of Gowrie. These two great monoliths are said to have figured in a rhyme by the seer Thomas the Rhymer: 'When the Goors of Gowrie come to land, Judgement Day is near to hand.' Perhaps the landfilling policy of the nearby city is of more importance than has generally been thought!

Another story of the same type comes from Strathpeffer (B11) in the Highlands and involves Finn MacCool himself. He was staying in a fort on top of Knockfarrel, nowadays overlooking Strathpeffer, when he was challenged to a stone-putting competition by a local giant renowned for his prowess. The mighty Finn felt this a bit beneath his dignity so he offered to pit his dwarf against Stoneputter. The competition took place on Knockfarrel itself. The giant lifted a stone which three men together could not lift and he threw it into the valley. This was the Eagle Stone, the Pictish symbol stone just to the east of the village. Then it was the dwarf's turn. He went to the two gateposts of the old fort of Knockfarrel, each of which was too heavy for seven men to lift, and threw them singly to stand on either side of the Eagle stone. Even Finn's dwarf was superior to the local giant! The proof of the story is that one of these stones supposedly has the marks of a finger and thumb on it.

Granish Moor

On Granish Moor (B26) just north of Aviemore there is a small loch called Loch nan Carraigean (B27), loch of the stones, from where a tradition comes which may have inspired the witch scene in Shakespeare's *Macbeth*.

Granish Moor

The freshly-crowned king of the Picts was said to have come to consult at this circle of stones with the three women who lived there. The spirits were then raised by some kind of ritual and asked about the future of his reign. The Picts are often presented as a semi-fictitious group, but they were simply a people otherwise referred to as Caledonians who inhabited Scotland from the time of the Romans until the ninth century. At that point, they merged with Gaelic-speaking Scots to form the new kingdom of Scotland. Macbeth, who seems to have been an honourable and efficient king with an excellent claim to the throne of Scotland, came from Moray, long the heartland of the northern Picts and a continuing source of trouble for the centralizing Scottish kings of the early Middle Ages. Presumably it was the kings or leaders of these tribes who came to Loch nan Carraigean.

Lang Man's Grave

In the lonely glen below Macbeth's one-time castle on Dunsinane (D21) there is a strange stone with an even stranger story attached to it. The stone, which once appears to have been a standing stone, is lying on the ground on the north side of the road from Balbeggie to Abernyte, just east of the burn which runs down between Dunsinane and Black Hill. The stone itself lies under the roadside dyke. For many years the roadmen cleaned the small gravel bed surrounding the stone on the roadside to show respect for our ancient traditions. The stone is associated with the Lang Man, a weel-kennt and successful horse trader who regularly visited the annual fair held in the glen. Standing about two metres tall he was a gregarious character, and one of the great delights of the fair was said to be having a dram with the Lang Man. Tradition does not give us a date for the story but we are told that one year the Lang Man disappeared and when the fair was over his tent still stood, his horse tethered beside it. Of the Lang Man himself there was no sign. There had been no suggestion of trouble or violence beyond the normal drunken boisterousness of the fair, so rumours of witchcraft ran rife. No one was prepared to take down his tent, though the horse was soon appropriated. The wind and weather came to destroy the flapping canvas of his tent and the tale began to spread that he had been murdered for his poke o gowd and buried beneath the great stone lying by the road. Perhaps we will never know if anyone lies in the Lang Man's Grave (D22) but its proximity to Dunsinane and the reverence shown to the stone itself have led to suggestions that this is where the original Stone of Destiny was buried when it was taken away from Scone at the approach of the English army in 1296.

Calanish

One of the most remarkable megalithic structures in Britain and Ireland stands overlooking Loch Roag (A3) on the western side of the Isle of Lewis. This is the unique stone circle of Calanish. The landscape around it is dotted with many more megalithic sites, showing that this was an area of major importance five thousand years ago. The location of the site by a sea loch at one of the western fringes of Europe reminds us that travel by water was commonplace then, and much easier than travel across the heavily wooded land mass of the continent. The monument is roughly in the shape of a Celtic cross: there is a central circle, a long avenue running north/south and shorter avenues leading from the circle to east and west, although the original design is no longer totally extant, some stones having disappeared.

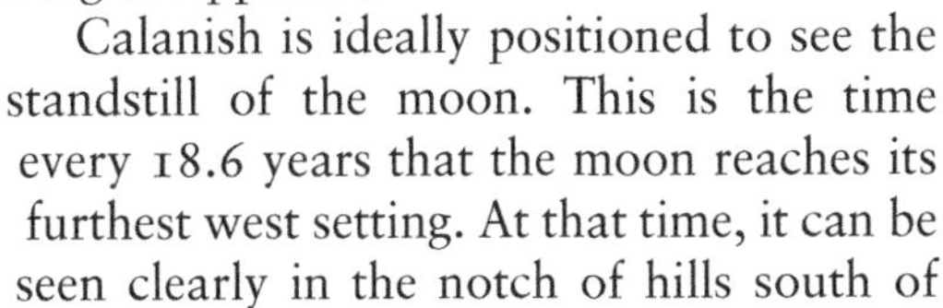

Calanish

Calanish is ideally positioned to see the standstill of the moon. This is the time every 18.6 years that the moon reaches its furthest west setting. At that time, it can be seen clearly in the notch of hills south of the avenue of Calanish. The hills to the south are *Cailich na Mointich*, discussed above with reference to the shape of a sleeping woman.

When Martin Martin visited the island in 1695 he was told that the site had been a place of worship in heathen times. He was not the first to write of this mysterious and awesome place however. An ancient Greek writer wrote of a priest called Abaris who came to Athens around 350 AD from 'the winged temple of Apollo' in Hyperborea. Hyperborea means 'place beyond the north wind' and is generally agreed to refer to the British Isles. Many scholars feel that the reference is specifically to Stonehenge, but Calanish is a much better fit. The god Apollo was said to dance at this temple every nineteen years and we have already seen how Calanish was created to watch the 18.6 year cycle of the moon. But Apollo is a sun god, anyway. And here the local legends of Calanish begin to matter. Each Midsummer 'the shining one' is said to walk down the central avenue of Calanish. He is heralded by a cuckoo (and it was thought that all cuckoos visiting Lewis first flew to Calanish). While 'the shining one' is usually though to be Lugh, it might also be a reference to Apollo.

A legend concerning the erection of the stones was written down by a local minister last century and it tells of a group of ships coming into Loch Roag manned by black men. They were accompanied by priests, the chief of whom had a white cloak of bird feathers. After the stones were erected, the ships and their crews left but the priests stayed behind to officiate at the stones. All we know by way of background to this tale is that the megalith builders seem to have sailed up the coast of Europe from as far south as Morocco. All the Atlantic coastal lands have great stone creations and it is intriguing that many of them are from Morocco.

Calanish has attracted other types of more general stories through its long existence. One story says that local giants met to discuss what to do about the arrival of a Christian missionary – St Kieran – who turned them into stone once they had all gathered!

Another story tells of a great white cow that came to the stones from Loch Roag in a time of hardship and near famine after a Viking raid on the island. No matter how often she was milked this cow gave freely to everyone who brought a pail. One day a woman came with two pails and the cow asked her (in Gaelic) what she was doing. The woman explained that her friend was sick and had asked her to bring her pail for milk. So the cow let her have two pails' worth of milk. This was noticed by another woman, who happened to be a greedy witch. She brought two buckets the next day, but the cow realised what was happening and only let her have the one. Angered by this, the spiteful witch returned the following day with one pail – but it was a pail with no bottom. In this way she milked the cow dry and the magical creature disappeared, never to be seen again.

Another local tale of witchcraft concerns two young women who were in love with the same man. They had been friends but were now being driven apart. One of them went to consult a witch as to how she could ensure her success. The witch gave her a magic belt which she was to give to her rival. She would then be taken away by her 'master' – the Devil. The lass accepted the belt but began to realise what she was doing; she decided against harming her friend. But how could she get rid of her belt?

She went on her own late one evening to the stones of Calanish. Summoning all her courage, she took the belt and fastened it around one of the stones. The stone burst into flame and the air was filled with a great noise of howling and honking and the flapping of wings. A great cloud of smoke began to gather and the lass took to her heels. But the next day she returned. The stone round which she had fastened the belt was broken just above where it had been clasped and the upper half of it lay on the ground with scorch marks at the break. This is believed to be the stone just outside the circle on the east side of the southern avenue, given as number 34 in some descriptions.

The range of stories relating to Calanish is hardly surprising. When you first see them along the ridge at Breasclete (A2) they take your breath away. As more and more sites in the locality are discovered, the fundamental importance of this magical place is underlined.

Standing stones and circles have been associated with many kinds of activity over the past few decades. Some people see them as markers on a system of ley lines – lines of electro-magnetic power that run vast distances across the landscape, absolutely straight. Others think of them as some kind of geo-physical acupuncture for the planet. Still others think they provide the focus for extraterrestrial activity, while others use them for their own version of re-invented paganism. What this clearly illustrates is that these megalithic remnants have lost none of their psychological attraction for us. The legends associated with them show just how divergent the rituals and beliefs surrounding them have been.

CHAPTER 11

Wells, Trees and Sacred Groves

WATER IS BASIC TO SCOTLAND. We have lochs, rivers, wells and springs – and rain in all our seasons. But water is also the bearer of sanctity and is involved in the rituals of many religions. Christians use water for baptism and christening. Water was also at the heart of various earlier religions. The association of goddess-type figures with our rivers attests to this. In pagan times water may have been seen as the blood of a goddess.

In Scotland many well-rituals survived into the nineteenth and twentieth centuries, giving us glimpses of how our ancestors saw themselves in the world. Many of these wells have been, and some continue to be, associated with healing.

Nine Maidens Wells

We have read about Martin's Stane and the nine maidens. The same nine crop up in other locations and an almost identical story is told of a well at Kildrummy (B50) near Castle Forbes in Aberdeenshire. Here the founder of Clan Forbes, a Pictish warrior called Ochonochar, slew a great wild boar which had also killed nine maidens. Other nine maidens wells can be found at Cortachy, (D8) Finavon (D10), Glamis (D13), Newburgh (D45), Tough (B49) and Pitsligo (B23), Loch Tay, Parkside (by Murrayshall (D24)) and in Abernethy on the south of the Tay, east of Perth. There is a possibility that many of the Ninewells that exist all across Scotland were at one time nine maidens wells, though there are other valid interpretations of the name. At Abernethy, the nine maidens were said to be the companions of St Brigit who came over from Ireland at the request of the Pictish king to set up a nunnery.

The motif of the nine maidens exists in the mythology and lore of most Western European countries, possibly linking such diverse figures as King Arthur, the Norse gods Heimdall and Odin, Apollo and the Welsh St Samson of Dol.

Nine Maidens Well

Bride's Wells

Bride (and St Brigit) were often associated with well-rituals. One such survived until recently at Bride's Well at Sanquhar (C3) in the Southwest. Here, young women would go to the well at Beltane and place nine white stones in it. (The link to the nine maidens theme is attractive, but the use of white pebbles is equally striking. White pebbles were used by both pagans and early Christians as talismans to be placed into graves.)

There are Bride's Wells all over Scotland from Wigton (C1) to Aberdeen and one particular one at Pitlochry was said to provide a cure for respiratory diseases. Another Bride's Well at Corgarrf, between Braemar and Tomintoul, was a favourite spot for brides. On the evening before their marriages it was customary for young girls to go to the well with their bridesmaids, who would bathe the bride's feet and the upper parts of her body with water from the well. It was believed that this bathing would ensure the girl a family.

Clootie Well

The best-known Clootie Well (B13) is on the Black Isle. Here, the trees on both sides of the well alongside the road are draped with rags. This is a remnant of belief in a healing well. A rag would be tied by a sufferer to the holy tree beside the well and as the rag faded so the affliction would disappear. This applied to sicknesses of the heart and mind as well as of the body. It was also acceptable for people to take rags on behalf of others too ill to move. Of

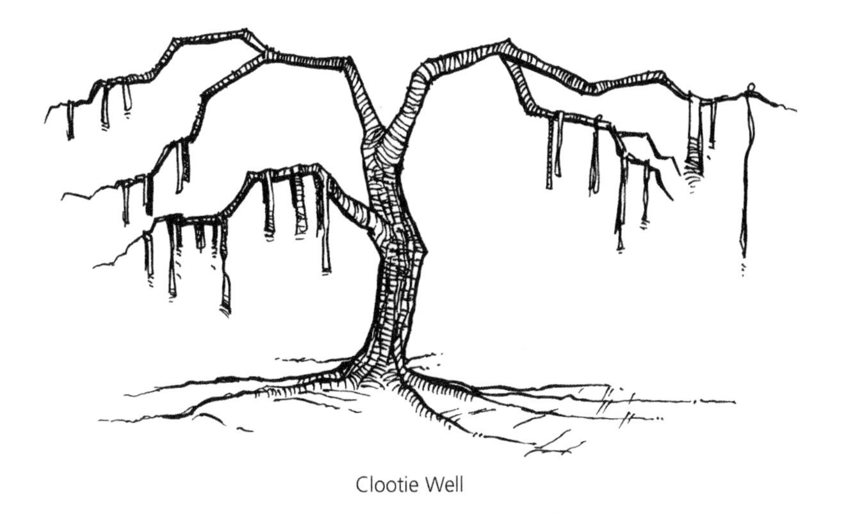

Clootie Well

course anyone mad enough to remove or meddle with the rags would fall heir to all the diseases represented! Such practices were widespread and a particularly well-known Clootie Well is on Culloden Moor, sadly famous for other things.

Like so many of the healing wells, this one was visited at Beltane. It seems that such pilgrimages could become great social occasions in which, as in pagan times, religious practice and revelry would be totally intermingled. The Clootie Well on Culloden (B14) was also known as St Mary's Well, The Blue Well and *Tobar n' Oige*, or well of youth. This last name suggests a link to that fabulous land *Tír nan Óg*, the land of youth which occurs in early Gaelic literature and folklore. The ritual at this well is likely to have been pretty much consistent with that performed at others. The pilgrim would walk three times 'sunwise' (clockwise) round the well then drink from it with cupped hands while making his wish or prayer. Then a piece of silver would be thrown into the well. Finally the pilgrim would tie a rag of clothing to the branch of the overhanging tree or bush. This was thought by some to immediately remove all ill-health. The entire ritual had to be performed in silence before the sun rose. Certain wells have updated ancient practice and have charity boxes for donations.

Eye Wells

Many wells in Scotland are said to have been a particular source of remedies for ocular ailments. Some of these 'eye wells' are dedicated to early saints like St Triduana and St Monenna. The latter was said to have been accompanied by nine maidens and a boy. The stories of St Triduana and St Monenna are essentially the same. St Triduana, despite having entered the sisterhood of nuns and dedicating her life to Jesus, was pursued by an ardent suitor who, in true early Christian style, was of royal descent. Try as she might, she could not escape from him. She moved several times but still he came after her, despite her strict vow of chastity. At last she asked him what it was about her that most attracted him. On being told that he was enflamed by her beautiful eyes she simply plucked them out and gave them to the astonished prince. This is said to be why certain wells were good for the eyes. St Triduana's Well in Edinburgh was originally at Restalrig Church in Edinburgh but was moved to a location in Holyrood Park (D58) where it can still be seen opposite Holyrood Palace. What is truly remarkable about St Monenna is that she is reported to have had churches dedicated to her on Traprain Law (D55) in East Lothian, Edinburgh Castle Rock (D59), Stirling Castle Rock (D37), Dumbarton (C9) and Dundonald (C4) in Ayrshire. All of these were heavily fortified sites and almost certainly tribal capitals in the Dark Ages.

Moving Wells

On the island of Islay there is a well that is said to have originated on Colonsay (C20). One day a local woman went to the well and washed her hands in it. This sacrilegious act was outrageous and the well immediately spirited itself away to Islay where ever after it was properly respected and was the site of numerous pilgrimages.

Another version of the same story tells that the well was brought to Islay by Donald, Lord of the Isles, when he moved from Colonsay to Finlaggan (C21) in Islay. Other movable wells seem to have shifted for the same kind of reason but there is one story of a moving well that takes some beating.

The story is from Strath Dearn (B24), southeast of Inverness (B15). A man who had been raised here by the headwaters of the Findhorn River grew old watching his friends and relatives leave their beloved Highlands for a better life on the Canadian prairies. Despite regular invitations he declined to follow them and lived on in Strath Dearn. One of the things that kept him there was his attachment to the well near his birthplace which had supplied him with water all his days. However, after many years his relatives at last convinced him to go to Canada. He went to the well for the last time and sat on the large white rock where he often read his Bible. He was still thinking of the spot when he arrived in Canada. And there, just a few yards from his new home was his faithful well and the white boulder waiting for him.

The Queen and the Well

Wells are magic in many ways and crop up in all sorts of stories. This one comes from Port Ellen (C22) on Islay. One day the queen fell ill and told the eldest of her daughters to go to the Well of True Water to bring her a drink. She was sure that this would restore her to health. On reaching the Well of True Water the young princess was approached by a large frog who asked her to marry him. She was mortally offended at the suggestion and said she would never do such a thing. 'Well then,' said the toad, 'You'll not get any water.'

On returning home without the water the queen was angry and sent the girl's younger sister to the well instead. The same thing happened to the second sister as had happened to the first and she too came home without any water.

By this time the queen was very ill. In desperation she sent her youngest daughter to the Well of True Water to bring her a drink. When she got there the frog appeared again and asked the third sister if she would marry him. On being told that this was the only way he would let her have the water for her mother, the lass agreed to wed the frog. He gave her the water and she ran off at once to her mother. The queen drank the water and immediately felt better.

That night after all were in bed, the frog came to the front of their dwelling and called to the youngest sister: 'Gentle one, gentle one, remember the pledge you gave me beside the well, my love.' He kept repeating this over and over and at last the princess came down and let him in, putting him behind the door. She went back to bed but soon was awakened by the frog repeating that same phrase over and over again. So she took him into her chamber and put him down there. It was not long before he started again, repeating and repeating the same phrase. She then made him a wee bed right by the fire hoping this would quieten him. But again he started and this time she made him up a bed alongside her own. Yet again he started but she decided enough was enough and ignored him. At that his chant stopped and he said to her, 'There is an old rusty sword behind your bed. Lift it up and cut off my head, rather than that this torture should go on.'

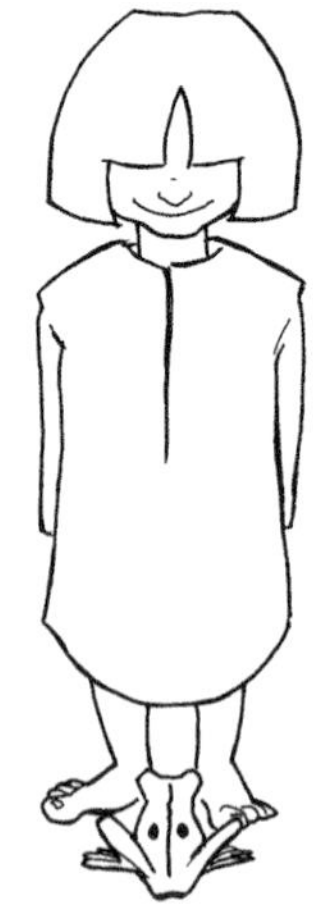

The Queen and the frog

So she took up the old rusty sword and with a clean stroke cut off the frog's head. Then there in front of her stood a handsome young man. He told her his story: he was a king from a nearby kingdom who had been put under a spell and as she had saved his life by agreeing to marry him they could now be wed. The young princess was very taken by the handsome stranger and soon they were married and had a long and happy life together.

Katherine's Well

As we have seen, the pre-Reformation church was quite amenable to absorbing earlier religious practices into its own rituals. A striking example of this comes from Eigg (A26).

In the late eighteenth century Martin Martin toured the Western

Isles leaving us a remarkable record of his journey. According to him the water from the well on Eigg, known as Katherine's Well, was believed locally to be extremely beneficial. The natives told Martin that it had been so ever since being blessed by Father Hugh, a Catholic priest. He had gathered all of the inhabitants of the island at the well and got them to raise a huge cairn at the head of the well. He then blessed the well and gave all present a small piece of candle which they lit. The priest then led the assembled throng in single file 'sunwise' round the well. From then on it was sacrilege to use the water of the well for cooking.

This is clearly a remnant of an early practice which some priests saw as useful. Most wells were believed to be at the peak of their powers on Beltane or one of the other feast days – Samhain (1 November), Imbolc (1 February), or Lammas (1 August).

The modern idea of the 'wishing' well is clearly derived from this kind of ancient idea of supplication. One of the ongoing concerns in society in older times was fertility and there were many locations which were thought to have the power to make barren women fertile, or at least encourage the possibility of pregnancy. Naturally, some of these sites were wells.

The Well in Willie's Muir

John R. Allan was told the following story in the 1920s by an old man who saw the ritual when he himself was a young lad. The well concerned was located in an area called Willie's Muir in Aberdeenshire.

The well was in a sheltered dip on the moor and the water came out among some stones surrounded by whin-bushes. Three women of child-bearing age went to the well at Midsummer accompanied by an older woman who was clearly the one in charge. The young lad followed them, keeping in cover all the while.

On reaching the well and with instruction from the older woman, the three others took off their shoes and stockings and pulled their skirts and petticoats up to bare their bellies. They then circled the well three times sunwise, holding up their skirts as if holding themselves towards the sun. As they came round, the old woman cupped water from the well and splashed each one's genitalia with it. Not a word was spoken, even though the water must have been gey cold. Three times round they went and then the old woman made a sign. The women dropped their skirts and petticoats. Then they opened their dresses to the waist and pulled them down, freeing their breasts. At another sign from the Auld Wife, they knelt before her and this time she took the spring water and sprinkled it over their breasts three time three. Then they adjusted their clothing, put on their stockings and shoes and left. This report probably dates from the middle of the nineteenth century.

Sacred Trees

As mentioned above, the ancient holy wells were usually adjoined by one or more trees. The famous well of St Mourie on Isle Maree has such a tree which pilgrims used to shove or hammer coins in as a token of respect and to have good luck. There are stories of wells in Argyll that have nine hazel trees growing around them still. This is an echo of the motif in both Irish and Scottish Gaelic tales of the Well of Knowledge. This mystical well was surrounded by nine hazel trees whose nuts bore the sum of human knowledge. The nuts would fall into the pool and in the pool was a salmon who fed on the nuts, thus becoming immensely knowledgeable.

Trees can be significant either as individual entities or in groves and there are said to have been many trees that were seen as particularly sacred by the tribal peoples of Britain. The best known of these is the oak, with its links to the shadowy figures of the druids. There are records of mistletoe cut at Samhain being used to ward off witchcraft or to protect children from being stolen by fairies.

The Rowan

The most widely respected tree in Scotland was the rowan. Its berries were said to have been the food of the gods but its particular strength was in warding off evil. The wood of the rowan was used for the pins of ploughs, millstones, churn-staffs and pegs of cow-shackles. It was also common for the central cross-beam in the chimneys of old houses to be made of rowan. The term could also be used for the main roofbeam of a house. To ward off evil from one's cattle it was common to put a sprig of rowan over the byre door or even to tie sprigs of it to cows' tails, but always with red thread. An old rhyme tells of the efficacy of using red thread of wool, silk or linen, with the rowan:

> Rowan tree an red threid
> Gar the witches tyne their speed.

Rowan would only be used as firewood for the neid-fire or ritual cooking at Beltane and other special times. The rowan or rodden tree was used at Beltane extensively. It has long been thought of as the most effective plant against witchcraft and black magic, which is why there is hardly a house in the Highlands that did not have a rowan tree growing at its front door at one time. With the depletion of the population of the Highlands solitary rowans may be seen on a hillside or in a glen where all that remains of a house is a rickle of stones.

The Yew

Perhaps the most significant of our indigenous trees is the yew. The great placename scholar W. J. Watson has suggested that the name 'Iona' derives from 'island of yews'. Throughout Scotland there are not only kirkyards with yews in them but even enclosed by yews or with yew-arches at their entrance. Perhaps the yew contains some active healing ingredient we have forgotten, as many of the sacred trees seem to have. Another possibility is that extracts of certain nuts or fruits could have been used to induce visionary trances. The reverence for the yew might derive from something much more obvious. It is a remarkably long-lived tree and as such could be seen to signify immortality or rebirth in either a pagan or Christian context.

Sacred Groves

The Romans wrote of nemetons, or sacred groves, in these islands and elsewhere. The name is reminiscent of Gaelic *neimheadh*, a sacred enclosure. The term was often used for precisely those previously sacred grounds in which so many early churches were raised. These nemetons were sacred spots which probably had judicial or social functions. They can be found in most areas of Scotland – Roseneath (C10) on the Gareloch, Nevay in Angus, Navidale (B7) in Sutherland, Slocknvata in the Rhinns of Galloway, Navitie in Fife and Craig Neimhidh in Glenurquhart.

Another of these ancient sites was Tarnavie (D43). This is a large mound nestling under Craig Rossie (D42) on the south side of Strathearn near Dunning (D44), one of the places where St Serf slew a dragon. The name Tarnavie was long thought to have come from *terra navis*, or ship of land, because of the shape of the hill: it is a bit like an upturned boat. There is an interesting tale about this site. At a date that no one has ever been certain about, a local farmer came to Tarnavie to dig up some sand. He knew he could get what he wanted there, perhaps because it was initially a drumlin, a mound caused by riverine action. He proceeded to dig. He had hardly started when in front of him he saw a very small man dressed in an old and outlandish style. The strange man asked him what he was doing and on being told replied, 'How would you feel if someone came along and started throwing the slates off your roof? You are disturbing my home. Begone with you now.'

At that the wee man simply sank back into the hill and the farmer turned to his heels and ran. He never set foot on Tarnavie again.

Whether this is a tale intended to frighten people off or to remind them of a fairy hill we cannot be sure. It is very like the ideas we looked at in Chapter 1, here linked directly to a name suggesting if not a sacred grove of trees, at least a sacred site or enclosure of some kind. Interestingly, Tomnahurich, which we looked at earlier, is Gaelic for hill of the yew trees. Folktales often contain ancient ideas of sanctity and reference to old holy sites in our landscape.

CHAPTER 12

And then ...

THE OXFORD ENGLISH DICTIONARY defines Myth as 'a purely fictitious narrative usually involving supernatural persons, actions or events, and embodying some popular idea concerning natural or historical phenomena'. This seems a trifle harsh as we can see all human religion as arising from mythology, and an alternative description might be that it is an attempt to explain the natural world, its origin and events in terms of human behaviour. Most mythology can be understood as having developed long ago, generally amongst pre-literate peoples, and given the nature of ancient society it is little wonder that the world was explained through the activities of supernatural beings who were largely based on human types. The idea of the supernatural itself is a way of dealing with the often confusing and mysterious aspects of life. Nowadays we tend to rely on 'scientific' explanations, but as we have seen often enough, these too can turn out to be based on little more than articles of faith. An example of this is the reliance that developed societies put on nuclear power as the answer to energy problems in the second half of the twentieth century. Chernobyl, Three Mile Island and other instances of malfunction have shown the problems nuclear power creates, yet there are still those who claim it is the answer to mankind's energy requirements. Pollution, environmental degradation and ever increasing levels of conditions like asthma in the most developed countries suggest our 'scientific' approach to the world and its challenges might not be the answer. Yet our leaders' faith in progress appears undimmed. In one sense this idealised concept of progress is a modern mythology, and the religion deriving from that myth is the worship of money.

The mythological pantheons of Greece and Scandinavia are well documented and there have been many attempts to define a

'Celtic' mythology as well. In so far as Scotland has, or even had, a mythology, it has always been interpreted as essentially little more than a hand-me-down from original Irish sources. This is no longer tenable and I suggest here that there are in fact enough remaining stories and other remnants from the past to make the case for an indigenous mythology which, though related to other beliefs, is effectively Scottish.

As the new millennium began, people all over the world sang Auld Lang Syne, a song given its form by the Scottish poet Rabbie Burns. And as we crossed our arms and linked hands we were taking part in a remnant of an ancient ring dance older than anyone can compute. There is an old saying in Scots, 'Gin ye dinnae ken whaur ye've been, hou can ye tell whaur ye're gangin?', that can be translated as 'you must know where you've been if you want to know where you're going'. In today's world the electronic media seems to be ever more obsessed with what is going to happen tomorrow, and incredible amounts of financial and human resources are devoted to the creation of new fads and fashions. Cultures from all over the world are pillaged for 'new' ideas in art, fashion and music. We are certainly not the first humans to think of ourselves as modern, but in the thinking of the developed industrial capitalist system that has been forced on the world by dominant Western powers over the past four hundred years, we are perhaps the first humans to be in danger of completely cutting ourselves off from our past. We are constantly presented with novelty for novelty's sake. Hand in hand with this is another equally inane obsession – youth. We are all supposed to be eternal teenagers. All of this arises not from a deep human need but from a simple greed for profit by the dominant organisations of our world – large-scale corporations and their minions, who have corrupted democracy by putting their interests before the interests of those who they claim to represent.

However, the last couple of decades have seen a reaction against this type of thinking, a reaction that can be clearly seen in the ever-developing interest in all aspects of our history. And in Scotland there is a further dimension to this. The Scottish Parliament, brought into being by popular demand, has given rise to a new-found sense of confidence. It is, however, one of the great anomalies of contemporary Scottish society that though the world knows of many aspects of Scottish culture, we are still afraid to teach Scottish history and culture to our children in any systematic fashion. Little Scottish history is taught, and in terms of Scots language and culture, often all the little ones get is a week of Scots literature around the anniversary of Robert Burns's birth. It seems the senior school curriculum is still essentially dictated by the demands of a defunct empire that equated interest in Scottish culture with a wish for political separatism. The result has been a distorted idea of Scottish history and culture. As long as this continues there will be a reaction against a British view of history that ignores what it does not like and distorts what it cannot ignore.

Thus far we have been looking at traditional tales from all over Scotland. Is it at all possible that the oldest tales, or the tales associated with the oldest sites, have enough in common to allow us to perhaps see the outline of an indigenous Scottish mythology? I believe there is. There are similarities in tales that have survived about megalithic sites – the oldest recognisable human artefacts in our landscape – and in tales that are directly associated with the landscape itself. Modern research in various fields has opened up the possibility of looking at such ancient orally-transmitted material in new ways that can advance our understanding not only of the far past, but of the development of the human story in Scotland since the Stone Age. Many writers in the past have stressed the ethno-linguistic aspect of much of Scotland's culture, some even going so far as to say the true indigenous reality of our culture comes from Gaelic speaking communities alone. I believe this to be wrong in light of what we now understand about Scotland's past. In a remarkable book, *An Archaeology of Natural Places,* Professor Richard Bradley of Reading University describes places in the natural landscape of different societies that became the focus of sacral behaviour. As we shall see this has a particular resonance in Scotland. An article in the magazine *Antiquity*, a similarly seminal work by Ewan Campbell of Glasgow University's Department of

Archaeology, looked at the evidence for the long accepted founding of the Scottish political entity (the use of the word kingdom is not one I find accurate enough in this situation) of Dalriada, by invaders from Northern Ireland. Just as the invasion theories of former years – such as that of the Beaker People and even the Anglo-Saxons into England – have long been challenged, Campbell has now looked at the archaeological, linguistic and historical evidence for this invasion and found there to be none. I find the arguments persuasive and think that we can learn much by concentrating on evidence from within Scotland to develop a picture of our past. A past that is not dependent on written sources all too often originating from outside Scotland.

While traditional orally transmitted material may not provide dates, personalities and definable actions, it does not suffer from the limitation of human history, which is simply that history is always written on behalf of somebody. The alternate views of the Second World War propounded by American and Russian historians provide a good example of this. They describe the same events but not in the same way, because they are driven by imperatives other than the story of what happened. Those imperatives are political. Just as there has been a tendency to exaggerate the influence of Ireland in our past, so the influence of Scandinavia has been minimised, and where it is accredited has often been presented as essentially different from the so-called 'Celtic' culture we are supposed to have inherited from Ireland. This latter idea is as irrelevant as the ridiculous notion that the Germanic language that developed into modern Scots was brought here at the time of Malcolm Canmore in the eleventh century. We know that some of the soldiers of the Roman army on their brief incursions into Scotland were Germanic speakers, and that in the fourth century there was an alliance between Germanic-speaking tribes, the Picts and Scots, who attacked Hadrian's Wall together. The alliance could hardly have been formed overnight and the archaeological record again shows that there have been cultural contacts between Scotland and Scandinavia and Mainland Europe since megalithic times. When

Calanish was being raised we should also remember that the pyramids in Egypt had not yet been thought of.

None of this is to suggest that Scotland has been impervious to outside influence, but simply that the idea of our culture developing in the main because of outside influence is insulting to our ancestors. I would go so far as to say that due to frequent arrivals, not invasions, of people from other places we are essentially a mongrel race, and all the better for it. The idea of 'the Celtic nations', which has found so much support of late, is a post-Union idea and is much to do with reaction against the overbearing aspects of British, meaning essentially English, culture that arose after the Union.

The idea of Celtic ethnicity is in fact close to racism. No one in any of the Celtic-speaking countries three hundred years ago would have even understood the term as applied to ethnic origin or anything else, and its original use was a term describing a specific branch of languages. To hold that people are of a specific ethnicity because of the language they speak is nonsense. Many cultures on this planet of ours are polyglot – they speak several languages – and it is only the Western imperialist model of human development that suggests monoglot culture is the norm. That language is defined politically rather than linguistically is almost impossible to refute and can be summed up in the old cliché that a language is just one dialect with an army and a navy.

Some of the stories we have already looked at have clearly originated so long ago as to make even guessing what kind of language they were originally told in futile. This is not to say they have nothing to tell us. Stories survive language shifts and in Scotland we know of several of these. The language(s) spoken by the Picts, the Gododdin of south-east Scotland, and the Britons of Strathclyde, are now considered to have been related dialects of P-Celtic, akin to Old Welsh. These were superseded by Gaelic and Scots in ways that we do not yet fully understand. The old notion that this was a result of invasion by Germanic speakers – Angles, Saxons and Jutes – is not one that receives scholarly support these days. Given the Celtic bias of so much Scottish history over the past few centuries we have tended to overplay the importance of the west of the country and one example illustrates this well. In the ancient Irish saga, the Wooing of Emer, the great Ulster hero Cuchullin is sent to Scotland to be trained and given arms by Scathach, a redoubtable female warrior on an island. Time and again this has been reported as having happened in Skye. In fact in the original source the island is said to be on the east of Scotland, and as I have suggested elsewhere (McHardy, 2003), the most likely option is the Isle of May in the Forth estuary.

The idea of female warriors is not unique and again some recent research supports the long-rejected notion that the Picts, dominant in the east and north of Scotland for a considerable period, might well have had a matrilinear system of succession. Here the apparently supreme male, generally referred to as a king, obtained his position by marrying the local queen who represented the sovereignty of the people who occupied the land. Such ideas are known elsewhere, including Ireland, and could account for the fact there are no instances of a Pictish king succeeding his father, a system we have long been presented with in history as the norm.

Another telling aspect of our culture that has been under-appreciated is the role of tribalism in Scottish society. The Scottish Highland clans were a direct development of earlier tribal systems, systems that appear to have been the norm across the entire country until the advent of Christianity in the post-Roman period. Certain aspects of the Scottish Highland clan system, such as the insistence on the warrior tradition, a form of elective succession for the chiefs, the central economic importance of cattle, the absolute importance of kinship, suggest continuity with tribal societies of the distant past. And that continuity continued until the end of the clan society in the eighteenth century. In the classic texts on 'Celtic' society written in the second half of the twentieth century, Ross's *Pagan Celtic Britain*, Rees and Rees's *Celtic Heritage* and Dillon and Chadwick's *Celtic Realms* – which all purport to look at Celtic-speaking society in these islands – make scant reference to Scotland being the home of the longest lasting Celtic-speaking warrior society. This, despite the fact that the oldest known poem in the language now known as Welsh was written by and about warriors from Edinburgh and their kin. The Goddodin, the Strathclyde Britons and the Picts were all Celtic-speaking warrior societies, and as mentioned, the much-maligned theory of matrilinear succession amongst the Picts is nowadays gaining more support.

It is in fact in this female or feminine aspect that I perceive a basis for understanding what would appear to be an indigenous and unique Scottish mythology, though as in all areas of human activity there are always similarities with other cultures. Few human societies have ever lived in total isolation.

Calanish

As mentioned earlier the magnificent megalithic stone setting of Calanish (A4) is the focus of several tales. The Roman geographer Strabo mentioned a 'winged-temple of Apollo in Hyperborea' where the god Apollo danced every 19 years. Archeo-astronomy has discovered that Calanish was set up to monitor and observe the 18.6 year cycle of the moon, and Apollo has strong lunar associations. Hyperborea was the land beyond the north wind and though there have, of course, been suggestions that Strabo must have meant Stonehenge, Calanish seems a very good match. Apollo's mother, Leto, was said to have come from Hyperborea. There are other links between Scottish tales and Apollo, but for the moment I would like to consider the hills to the south of Calanish. There is a gap in the hills through which the moon can be seen from Calanish to set on two successive nights every 18.6 years. A local name of this range of hills is, as already noted, *Caillich na Mointich*, the Old Woman of the Moors. Here we have a major, astronomically accurate structure from over five thousand years ago, aligned on what is clearly to be understood as a reclining female figure in the landscape. In one local tradition the stones themselves are said to have been raised by several boatloads of black men who came from the south and departed after putting them up, leaving behind a priesthood who carried out rituals at the stones.

Whether this is precisely true or not we should remember that the megalithic culture did stretch down to North Africa, and that travel from there to the Hebrides up the Atlantic littoral would have been eminently possible.

What is intriguing here is that the figure in the landscape is female, not male. Many scholars have suggested that our oldest form of godhead is female; probably because of the female's childbearing role they are the creators and bearers of life. In modern times the concept of an all-encompassing female godhead has resurfaced in the notion of GAIA, the planet earth as a living entity of which we humans are but part. So is this female figure related to the idea of the Mother Goddess, found in so many societies, and can we find more evidence of her?

The Cailleach

The *Cailleach*, of which *Cailich* is variant, is the Hag of Winter as known in Scotland and Ireland, though there are many more stories and place names associated with her in the former name, as was painted out by the folklorist Katherine Eleanor Hunt over 50 years ago. The idea that the Cailleach was imported into Scotland from Ireland is another instance of reality contradicting accepted notions. If the Cailleach did in fact originate in Ireland why do we in Scotland have so many more stories about her? Her name in Gaelic means 'the hooded or veiled one' and after Christianity arrived became the accepted term for a nun. This has led to an interesting situation where confusion arises between a figure who was part of ancient Mother Goddess belief and Christian nuns. In ancient belief she was particularly known for spreading the harsh weather of winter and for living on mountain tops.

Within oral tradition people told the stories of their mythology and legend within their own environment and thus there are Cailleach stories and placenames in much of Highland Scotland and in many of the Hebridean islands. In the east of Scotland, where the Scots language developed parallel to Gaelic, she is known as the Carlin, who is sometimes said to have been the Queen of the Witches.

The later, Christian use of the name Cailleach to mean 'nun' clearly arises from the hooded wimples nuns wore, but in terms of the original Cailleach the idea of hooding or veiling has another meaning. A mountain top wreathed in cloud can be considered veiled. Local weather lore throughout Scotland, and still extant in some parts, is full of references to cloudy summits having a 'cap' on, i.e. with a hood or veil. Mountains on which the Cailleach was said to have lived include Ben Nevis, Ben Wyvis (D10), Ben Breac, Ben Cruachan (C24), the Paps of Jura (C19) and Schiehallion; and Lochnagar (B42) has its *Allt-na-Cailleach*, a burn, and *Caisteil Caillich*, her castle. There is also, of course, *Beinn na Caillich* in Knoydart and another in Skye. These are all high, prominent hills, particularly Ben Nevis, the highest point on the British Isles. Such hills are often the focus of changing weather patterns and are regularly seen with clouds clustered around them, before the clouds spread out over the surrounding countryside. Such occurrences could have led to the interpretation of the Cailleach as the Goddess creating the weather.

Her role in bringing on winter includes a tale of her riding out from Ben Nevis with eight sister hags to hammer the frost into the ground. This grouping of nine mythological or legendary females is extremely widespread both within and outside Scotland and I have looked at it in detail elsewhere (McHardy, 2003).

The Cailleach is also in many places credited with creating the landscape – hills, islands, and other land formations. This is one of the basic ideas of mythology – it explains the physical world in human terms and is therefore probably truly ancient indeed. Most of the Cailleach placenames in the Highlands are up high and some, like on Lochnagar (B42), are part of a cluster of significant placenames and specific physical markers – the massif has two clear breast shaped peaks, Meikle Pap and Little Pap. Such peaks appear to have been the focus for various kinds of spiritual or sacral belief and activity in the far past. I shall consider this later.

Cailleach and the landscape

In many areas the Cailleach is mentioned as having shaped and sometimes actually created the landscape, particularly the hills and mountains. Hugh Miller in his *Scenes and Legends* tells of how the Cailleach carried a vast pannier on her back filled with earth and boulders with which she formed all the hills of Ross-shire. Specifically, while she was carrying this large basket, it suddenly gave way, the contents poured out on the ground in a heap and this became Ben Vaichaird. The same story is told in other places and is also given as an explanation for the origin of the Hebrides. All of these depend on the Cailleach being a giant figure, and in this creation of the landscape she is clearly not just a supernatural figure but the dominant one, i.e. the Mother Goddess herself. This idea of a giant figure corresponds to the figure in the hills south of Calanish, the Sleeping Goddess of Ben Cruachan (C24) and, I suggest, the Sleeping Giant of Benarty overlooking Loch Leven. There is also the figure of the Muilertach who could stand on the rock of Ailsa Craig off the Ayrshire coast with one foot while the other was on Arran. As we have seen, a bawdy variation of the Cailleach as land-maker occurs in the medieval Scots poem 'The Gyre-Carling', where she is said to have evacuated North Berwick Law (D54) from her bowels. In 'The Manere of the Cryinge of Nae Playe' the poet William Dunbar described how she 'spittit Loch Lomond with her lippis. Thunner and fyreflaucht flew fra hir hippis.' 'Fyreflaucht' here is lighting and the picture this evokes is a startling one.

The Cailleach and lochs

A story is told of the Cailleach who lived on Ben Cruachan in Argyll (C24). She was the guardian of a well and it was her job to place a great slab of stone over it at nightfall and take it off at daybreak. One day she was tired and fell asleep by the well before putting the slab on it. As the well overflowed, the sound of the waters breaking through the Pass of Brander awoke her, but it was too late to do anything. This resulted in the creation of Loch Awe, and the story tells us such was her sorrow and regret that she turned into a block of stone that can still be seen in the pass. Almost exactly the same story is told about the creation of Loch Ness and Loch Tay and Loch Eck in Cowal. It is tempting to see some remnant of ancient practice in the reference to the nightly placing of the stone over the well and its removal next morning.

Wells

Water is essential to all life on earth, and as such it is easy to see why ancient belief systems perceived it as the blood of the Goddess herself. Before we mechanised our planet we all relied on wells of one kind or another and many people in the world still do. There is something beautiful and a little awesome in seeing a spring bubbling up from the ground, even if today we think we can explain its appearance in terms of physical science. We cannot do the same of life itself. We have looked at several types of well already and it is noticeable that many wells are associated with supposedly early figures like St Bride, St Triduana and others, who appear to be Christianised versions of earlier figures. We know that certain wells were effectively taken over by the early Christians because they were already pilgrimage sites or healing wells. The Clootie Well in the Black Isle (B13) is still to this day a pilgrimage site, and although it is scruffy and a bit tacky, the constant addition of new materials, strips of cloth, whole articles of clothing, hats, shoes, poems and blessings underlines the fact that the concept of the holy well still holds a strong attraction for many people. The story of the well on Willie's Muir gives us a picture of an extant ritual practice that has clear pre-Christian origins and suggests, like the consistent visits to the Clootie Well – far from the population centres of Scotland – that continuities with the distant past continue.

The Cailleach's House

Another site of clearly pagan origin that we have not yet considered is the *Tigh na Cailliche* (C26) in Glen Cailliche to the north of *Beinn Mhanach* at the head of Glen Lyon in Perthshire. This is a miniature house containing three stones, representative of a mother, father and child, which are taken out of the house at Beltane and put back in at the end of the summer. The house is also rethatched every year. Its alternative name is *Tigh nam Bodach*, or Old Man's House, but *Bodach* is also used to describe phallic rock shapes in the landscape. Fertility, along with everything associated with it, was never a problematic issue for pagan religions, as it appears to have been for the sadly sin-obsessed Christians of Scotland's past. The site is at the foot of Glen Cailliche and it is perhaps its extreme remoteness that has allowed it to survive. Mention has been made in some books that there were originally twelve stones and that the site was dedicated to an early Christian saint. The shift of an initially Christian site to a site of pagan significance would be unique in Scottish terms, and it is more likely to be yet another example of an attempt at giving a Christian explanation for a pagan practice. The location of this site is extremely remote and difficult to access, but there were shielings used in the area till at least the end of the eighteenth century.

The Loathly Hag

The Cailleach is generally portrayed as a gigantic, ferociously ugly old crone. In several Scottish tales a wizened old hag comes to a group of the Fianna on a cold night in the hills, and asks by the laws of hospitality to be allowed to share a blanket with one of them. Finn MacCool and his son Oisin refused her, but Diarmaid let her share his blanket and she soon turned into a beautiful young maiden. By his kind action Diarmaid fulfils the true hero's role and the hag then appears to him in her true shape. Several scholars have seen in this story a link to other tales, in both Scotland and Ireland, where the sovereignty of the land was made manifest in a specific female. While this has strong echoes of the possible Pictish system of matrilineage the tale also suggest a duality in which the female figure is both the hag and the maiden.

The Corryvreckan Whirlpool

Earlier we looked at the story of the Cailleach washing her plaid in the Corryvreckan whirlpool (C17) between Jura and Scarba. Whirlpools are one of the most spectacular and awe-inspiring sights in nature. These magnificent spinning cauldrons are formed where tides crash or sea water is forced into narrow vortices. The Corryvreckan is one of only seven major whirlpools in the world. These magnificent examples of nature in the raw have long held a particular place in the human psyche, inspiring myths and legends in many cultures.

The Gulf of Corryvreckan is over 300 feet deep, but when the whirlpool is at full power a great cauldron is formed in the centre of it which is said to be measure over one hundred feet deep. The cause of this awesome power is a subterranean spike called *An Cailleach* off the coast of Scarba, which causes the great Atlantic waves to form into a giant vortex and create the Corryvreckan whirlpool. It is a dangerous place and local fishermen and sailors have countless stories of its hazards. Even on calm days the swell of the Corryvreckan can be several feet. The effect of the whirlpool is quite dramatic: for hour after hour when the Atlantic comes in, great spirals of water are thrown into the advancing tide. The spirals start with waves shooting up from a relatively flat surface with a great booming sound. When the whirlpool is at its wildest at the beginning of winter, the sounds can be heard more than 20 miles away.

The spirals thrown into the advancing Atlantic tide are just like those we find carved on megalithic sites in many parts of Europe, and it is not difficult to imagine the awe that this wonder of nature aroused in the hearts and minds of our ancestors. It is clearly significant that the spike that creates the whirlpool is called *An Cailleach*, and the Cailleach spreading her white plaid links the story to Ben Nevis. Here we have the most dramatic geophysical event in Europe and Britian's highest mountain linked in an ancient story through the person of the Cailleach. The mountain range to the south of Ben Nevis, the Mamores, part of the area said to be covered by her plaid, may also carry a link to the old beliefs in a Mother Goddess.

The Cailleach and deer

Traditionally the red deer of the mountains were known as the cattle of the Cailleach. A story told as recently as 1773 occurs in *Scrope's Days of Deer-stalking*, p.198ff. In this tale two hunters set out south from Braemar in search of red deer. They headed towards the forest of Atholl, but were overtaken by a snowstorm coming from the north which soon cleared. They managed to find some deer and shot and wounded a hind. As they trailed her by tracking the blood she had shed, the snowstorm returned, but this time much worse. Luckily they had their plaids with them and managed to find shelter in the lee of some rocks. They settled down to pass the night, eating the oatcakes and drinking the whisky they had brought with them. Come the morning things were little better and thoughts of hunting deer were replaced by the need to concentrate on one thing, survival. The wind was still blowing from the north and with visibility of no more than a few yards they could do little other than keep the wind at their backs as they struggled on. Unknown to them the wind began to veer to the east and keeping it at their backs meant they were heading west instead of south. There were no landmarks visible to help them at all. By nightfall their provisions were running out and they faced another night sheltering among rocks when they saw an old shieling bothy ahead of them. These were the traditional summer dwellings for the lads and lasses who went to the high pastures with the cattle after Beltane, and the hunters expected it to be deserted. Just as they came up to the bothy to their great surprise the door opened and there stood an old woman of wild and haggard appearance. Beckoning them in, she said she had been expecting them and that their supper and beds were ready. The hunters were astounded at this but went into the bothy. There they sat as the old woman, crooning a song in a language they did not recognise, poured out soup for them. Although they were cold and hungry, they realised that something uncanny was happening, and were reluctant to begin eating. The woman told them that she herself had power over the weather, and as they sat there petrified, she held up a rope with three knots in it and said :

> If I lowse the first [knot], there shall blaw a fair wind, such as the deer stalker may wish; if I lowse the second, a stronger blast shall sweep oer the hills; and if I lowse the third, sic a storm will brak out, as neither man nor beast can thole; and the blast shall yowl down the corries and the glens, and the pines shall faw crashin into the torrents, and this bare arm shall guide the course o the storm, as I sit on my throne of Cairn-Gower, on the tap o Ben-y-Gloe. Weel did ye ken my pouer the day, when the wind was cauld and dedly, and all was dimmed in snaw – and ye see that ye was expectit here, and ye hae brought nae venison; but if ye mean to thrive, ye maun place a fat hart, or a yeld [barren] hind in the braes o Atholl, by Fraser's cairn, at midnight, the first Monday in every month, while the season lasts. If ye neglect this my biddin, foul will befaw ye, and the fate of Walter o Rhuairm shall owertak ye; ye shall surely perish in the waste; the raven shall croak yer dirge; and yer bones shall be pickit by the eagle.
>
> (Scrope, 1773)

The hunters gave their word to do as she asked, ate and fell asleep, waking in the morning in a deserted bothy with no sign of the old woman. The storm had ceased and they made their way off the hill.

The old woman is clearly the Cailleach herself, and the knotted string links her to the various wise women who throughout the length and breadth of Scotland, sold winds to sailors into the nineteenth century. Although many of these women have been reported as witches it seems clear that their reputations among sailors were based on very old beliefs. The idea that the witches were the bearers of ancient traditions is much more likely than their being Satanists.

Scrope tells the story as if he believes it to be true, but it is reminiscent of ancient beliefs regarding the Cailleach. The are many locations throughout Scotland where she is closely associated with the red deer, and in the 1930s it was suggested that there was a deer-goddess cult and possibly deer-priestesses. Again this is something I have discussed elsewhere (McHardy, 2003) and it is worth noting that many Pictish symbol stones have deer carvings on them. Some are deer heads which look like masks and there are some grounds for thinking that there may indeed have been deer-priestesses in Scotland, perhaps performing rites like the one that still continues at Abbot's Bromley in Staffordshire, England. It is thought by many to be a survival of pagan practice. The dressing in deer skins, antlers, and other deer motifs, has been interpreted as a symbolic representation of shape-shifting, something which occurs amongst various female groups in traditional lore. Modern thinking associates this with the practices of shamanism, in which the practitioner 'becomes' another being to undertake a spirit journey. This type of belief is widespread and also very ancient.

On the side of one of the peaks of the Paps of Jura (C19) is the *Sgriob na Caillich*, the furrow or score the Cailleach carved down the side of Ben an Oir. Jura is famous for its population of red deer and the island's name comes from the Norse for 'Deer Isle'.

Additionally, stories about the great Gaelic hero Finn MacCool, many of which were long part of the traditional Gaelic lore of Western Scotland, frequently make reference to deer. Finn's original name was Demne, which has been interpreted as meaning 'little deer'. His first wife, Sadv, was changed into a deer by a malevolent Druid, and it was when pursuing her in this form, that Finn found his son Oisin, whose name means 'fawn'. Given the number and spread of the Finn MacCool stories they were clearly important to all the Gaelic-speaking people and this deer symbolism underlines the importance of the deer as a symbol within ancient belief in Scotland.

Bride

In one version of her story in Scotland, St Brigit, synonymous with Bride, is said to have come from Ireland to Abernethy with her Nine

Maidens at the behest of a Christian Pictish king. The truth is that the figure of Bride is common to much of the British Isles. She was originally a pagan goddess figure amongst many of the tribes living in mainland Britain as well as Ireland. In Scotland, Bride traditions appear to have merged with Christian iconography – for example, Bridget has been presented as present at the birth of Christ. We know that it was official Christian policy to take over pagan precincts and this is a case of an earlier important fertility figure, around whom many rituals focused, being grafted onto the new religion. This would have helped to make Christianity more accessible to and accepted by converts from paganism.

Although there is evidence to suggest that Bride was seen as a goddess by the Brigantes, a tribal grouping in northern England in the pre-Roman period, she is often said to have come into Scotland from Ireland. This is yet another idea which does not stand up to much scrutiny. The late medieval Scottish historian John Leslie said that though the Irish claimed Bride as their own, so did the Scots, who said she was buried at Abernethy on the banks of the Tay. Leslie is referring here to the supposed Christian St Bride or Brigit, but the earlier pagan figure in Scotland is significantly different from her counterpart in Ireland. The Scottish Bride is especially associated with the serpent or adder, while St Patrick supposedly cleared Ireland of snakes. In fact it seems clear there never have been adders, or any other snakes in Ireland. Snakes in general are associated with goddesses in many cultures, particularly as a motif of rebirth and fertility, and are also connected with Druids, underlining their importance in pre-Christian iconography. Their habit of sloughing their skin and apparently disappearing below ground throughout the winter months make them ideally symbolic of the notion of rebirth and regeneration. It is striking that adders occur regularly on the Pictish symbol stones from both the pagan and early Christian periods. There are ancient sites in the once Pictish parts of Scotland that are called Bride's Ring, Bed, and Coggie, in areas which were Christian-ised by the Columban church. One would expect them to be St Bride's names if this was when she was introduced. There is also a tradition, extant in the Abernethy area in the mid-nineteenth century, which has her coming to the Pictish capital of Abernethy from Glen Esk in Angus (D3), site of Bride's Bed. Just as the Brigantia tribe who lived in what is now north-eastern England claimed her as their own so it is clear she was essentially indigenous to Scotland, and her extensive links with the Nine Maidens underline that she was originally a pagan figure.

Bride locations

We have seen that the Cailleach is associated with mountains and hilltop sites throughout Scotland while most Bride or St Bride sites are in lower areas. This is not a Highland / Lowland division, for there are Bride sites in the Highland areas, but a matter of physical differentiation. Generally, on the mainland the Cailleach sites are high and the Bride sites are in glens and straths. We have seen that there are Bride's Wells in many parts of the country, and the Beltane ritual at her well in Sanquhar (C3) again appears to have strong pagan associations. Bride was also the focus of domestic rituals in Scotland, as we have seen, all of which underlines her importance in traditional belief. Although we do not have a fund of stories about Bride as we do for the Cailleach, her role as the focus of domestic activity amongst women suggests a significant role at the very heart of society. In many Highland communities on Bride's Eve an effigy of Bride was carried round every house by a group of young women dressed in white. This was followed by a feast of specially made food after which there was singing and dancing. The men of the community took a secondary role as little more than observers, but the ceremony was for everyone and appears pagan in origin.

Another ritual took place on Skye on Bride's Day, the first of February. It is recorded that a woman took a peat from her fire with a pair of tongs, then took off one of her stockings and inserted the peat into it. She then proceeded to pound it with the tongs, all the time intoning a verse about the queen coming forth from a mound. This is suggestive of some of the beliefs associated with fairies living in mounds, which may, as has been suggested, hearken back to ancient practices at the communal grave mounds at certain times of the year. Again it is clearly pre-Christian in origin.

Bride was closely linked with animals and as another practice demonstrates was also understood as the Goddess of Fertility. She was invoked in the ritual plucking of the torranan, or figwort plant, which was supposed to have beneficial powers for milking. By placing one of its flowers, plucked near the time of the high tide, beneath a milk-pail and circling *deasail* (sunwise) round the pail three times while chanting a verse to Bride, you would guarantee pails full of foaming milk and that the cream and cheese would be full of goodness and flavour. Like goddess figures all over the world here we have Bride right at the heart of society being invoked to help food production, and at a deeper level, survival.

Breast-shaped mountains

In different parts of Scotland in both Gaelic and Scots traditions we have place names that draw attention to female breast-shaped peaks in the landscape. The Gaelic term *cioch* – meaning a pap or nipple – is found in the name of Bennachie – *Beinn a' Cioch* – with its Mither Tap (B44), and Lochnagar (B42), which has both a Meikle and a Little Pap, and was also originally *Beinn na Ciochan*, the Hill of the Paps. Within what are generally regarded as Gaelic-speaking areas we have the Paps of Jura (C19) and the Pap of Glencoe (A23), while in Scots-speaking parts of the country there are the Paps of Fife, East and West Lomond Hill; the Paps of Lothian, North Berwick Law (D54) and Arthur's Seat; and Maiden Pap in Sutherland, another south of Hawick, one to the south-west of Dumfries, and smaller mounds called Maiden Paps (D63) in the Kilpatrick Hills. While it is obvious that these locations are so named because of their resemblance to the breast of a young female there are other aspects of these locations worth considering in light of what has been said about the Cailleach and Bride.

We have looked at instances of goddess forms in the landscape and should consider whether these breast-shaped geophysical locales might have had a role within the ancient pagan belief system. In his book *Scottish Hill Names* P. Drummond writes, '*Mam* has come to have the alternative meaning of a rounded hill, while *cioch* mountains generally come to a point, either in the apex of a cone, or in the nipple-like summit tors.' The *cioch* or Pap names refer to the breast shape of a young woman, while the mam name applies to more rounded shapes reminiscent of the older female form. At Bennachie (B44) we have Mither Tap, which I have recently heard was originally Mither Pap, Craig Shannoch which is a reference to the Shannoch Fires of Halloween, a variety of ancient monuments including the Maiden Causeway, and at the foot of the hill is the Maiden Stone (B43), a Pictish symbol stone. The tradition of Giant Johnnie Moir is linked to the other nipple shaped Aberdeenshire hill, currently called the Tap o Noth (B40) but which might earlier have been a Pap name too. A carved stone ball and a variety of stone axe heads, which were perhaps used ritually, have been found on or near the hill of Bennachie. Such a range of placenames, traditions and ancient monuments testify to the continuing importance of Bennachie to the local population.

At Lochnagar, *Beinn na Ciochan* (the Hill of the Paps), there are two Paps, *Allt-na-Cailleach*, and *Caisteal na Cailleach*, and at the foot of Meikle Pap is a well, now known by a Victorian name, the Fox Covert Well. There are no ancient monuments on Lochnagar, probably because it is such a wild place, and I know of no traditional stories associated with it. However Lochnagar has long been the site of pilgrimage to see the Midsummer sunrise for people all over the north-east of Scotland, and Midsummer was a significant day in ancient practice, just like Beltane and Halloween.

The Paps of Fife are East and West Lomond Hill. East Lomond is a breast-shaped hill with a fort in which a Pictish symbol stone of a bull was found. Between the two summits is a group of rocks formed like a natural altar with an early fish symbol on the central stone suggesting it was an early Christian site. The ridge running south from West Lomond Hill used to have a high stack of rock known locally as Carlin Maggie, reputed to have been a witch turned to stone by the Devil. Carlin of course corresponds to Cailleach. Also on the north-western slopes of West Lomond Hill is a natural rock formation known as the Maiden Bower. Here there is a channel through the rock which women used to crawl through in a fertility ritual. Maiden Castle, also on the north side of the Lomond Hills, is like some other similarly named sites in Britain in that it is clearly not a fortified site of any kind. The Maiden Pap south of Hawick (D63) is the site of a considerable number of ancient earthworks, including the Pict's Work Dyke or Catrail which extends for many miles. There is another Maiden Pap north of Helmsdale (B6) and another south of Dumfries. There are also Maiden stones which are striking coastal features at Eyemouth and Auchmithie on the east coast, which had ritual associations in the past. In addition there are Maiden Wells like the one near Dollar which was said to have been haunted by a beautiful, if dangerous, female spirit.

Harvest rites

In many parts of Europe we find terms that are connected with the end of the harvest and central to the Bride/Cailleach contrast. In Scotland the first sheaf of corn brought in at harvest was the 'Maiden', while the last sheaf was the 'Cailleach' or 'Auld Wife'. The Maiden sheaf was thought to bring good luck for the ensuing year, but the Cailleach sheaf brought the opposite. Each farmer kept his Maiden sheaf, but the first person to finish harvesting gave someone else his Cailleach sheaf, which would be subsequently passed on as farmers finished their harvests, as no one wanted to be the last person stuck with bad luck. In other parts of Europe the Maiden sheaf is known as the Bride. In the labelling of the Maiden and Cailleach sheafs we see a distinct contrast that echoes the polarity of the Cailleach, an ancient, malevolent and deadly hag who embodies winter and death, and Bride, a beautiful, fertile young woman who embodies summer and life.

Bride and the Cailleach

In the Cailleach we have at first sight someone who can have nothing to do with Bride. The Cailleach, so often associated with mountains, is portrayed in many parts of the country as a great black or blue faced hag whose primary function was to unleash winter upon the world. She is at another level clearly the Mother Goddess herself as can be seen in various stories of her creating the landscape – and there are remnants of her as part of the physical landscape in different parts of the country. She is associated with Ben Nevis, the dangerous and ever-changeable highest mountain in Britain, and the great whirlpool of Corryvreckan (C17) that presented other kinds of dangers for humans. Her name, 'the hooded or veiled one', is a good description of many of the mountains where she is said to have lived, looking after her cattle, the red deer.

While Bride is associated with the fertility of summer, the Cailleach is associated with the sterility of winter. Just as Bride is young and comely, the Cailleach is presented as an ancient and ugly crone. However there are traditions which link them together. The story of the crone changing to a beautiful young woman is echoed in another story which tells us that as the seasons were due to change the Cailleach, the oldest and first being, went to a specific well before dawn and drank of the waters. This turned her into beautiful Bride and took place just before sunrise on Beltane. Other stories tell of the Cailleach imprisoning Bride each year till she burst free in Spring. The oldest terms for the seasons in Scotland are the Time of the Big Sun (Summer) and the Time of the Little Sun (Winter), in which we can perhaps see another reference to Bride and the Cailleach as an ancient dual goddess belief system. Plotting the place names of the Cailleach and Bride shows that the former place names are generally in the mountains while Bride names proliferate in the glens, straths and lowland areas of Scotland. Like so many goddess figures around the world the Scottish goddess would appear to have been bi-polar, goddess of both winter and summer, barrenness and fertility, life and death. The traditional Scottish howdies, or midwives had a respected place in urban life into the twentieth century and apart from generally having healing knowledge also laid out corpses. It is tempting to see in their presence at both life and death a faint echo of the ancient belief in the goddess herself.

Masculine figures

The figure now generally known as 'King' Arthur was as much part of ancient P-Celtic tradition in Scotland as in Wales or Cornwall, and given his association with significant Scottish hills, e.g. the Eildons (D61), Ben Arthur, and Arthur's Seat there are some grounds for suggesting that he was, at one level at least, a mythical figure. He is associated with one particular female figure, Morgan, who is herself one of a group of Nine Maidens skilled in healing, prophecy and shape-shifting, suggesting they are pagan priestesses. Like Arthur, Finn MacCool and the Fianna in the Q-Celtic traditions are clearly at least semi-mythological heroes. Finn of course is linked strongly with the deer, which as we have seen, often occur in conjunction with goddess figures in traditional material. Both these great heroes occur in tales of sleeping warriors that might hark back to ancient practices at communal burial mounds. There are other shadowy masculine figures in stories of the Cailleach and we have of course Angus Og, from the mystical island of Tír nan Óg, the Land of Youth, who is said to have rescued Bride from the clutches of the Cailleach. However we seem to lack a pantheon of gods like the Greeks or Scandinavians. In both these mythologies the masculine figures predominate but at the most basic level we can still discern females who represent the fertility of the earth itself and probably derive from earlier, more central goddess figures.

Conclusion

One of the most striking aspects of Scottish working class culture through the twentieth century was the fascination with Scotland's mountains and hills. Nowadays hill-walking and all other mountain sports are big business, with hundreds of thousands of people heading off to the hills whenever they can. This dates from the 1930s when thousands of young Scots took to the hills, often with the most primitive of equipment. Our landscape is beautiful and people want to interact with it. From the top of Edinburgh's Arthur's Seat on a clear day you can see Schiehallion to the north-west, Lochnagar to the north, and Ben Lomond and Ben Arthur to the west. We are never far from the mountains and their beauty is such that visitors flock from all over the world to visit our country.

And it is in these mountains that the Mother Goddess was seen to have lived. We are not unique in having goddesses, or gods, sitting on our mountain tops. Such ideas are commonplace throughout the world. What is different is that we have till now paid so little attention to the tales of the Goddess associated with these peaks. Much work had been done, and is being done, on the early Christian period in Scotland, but there has been little research on pre-Christian belief systems. It is as if before Christianity, nothing mattered. It is all right to try to understand what happened in Greece and Rome, in Egypt and South America, but here we assume that before the Christian missionaries came we were a *tabula rasa*, a blank canvas, waiting for people more sophisticated, more intelligent, more capable than ourselves to come and teach us how to live and to think. This in the country where our ancestors raised Calanish (A4), Maes Howe (B1) and thousands of other amazing early sites of sanctity five thousand years ago and more. In Pictish art we have not only an indigenous body of creativity as wonderful as any in the world, but also the precursor of much of what has been called Insular Celtic Art. Some recent research now sees links between Stone Age carvings and some Pictish symbols – a continuity that is anything but impossible. We cannot see where we are going till we know where we have been, and the map we have of our past here in Scotland has been scribbled over too often by others' hands.

In order to know who we are and where we have come from we need to stop accepting other people's ideas of who and what we are. Just as the Highlanders were not bloodthirsty savages intent only on robbery and rapine, so our ancestors were not ignorant, unsophisticated buffoons – our archaeological record tells us clearly that they were anything but. Nor were they isolated from the world, an idea first propagated by Tacitus, a Roman. The importance of water, rivers and seas as an advantage, not a hindrance, to travel and communication, is only now beginning to be appreciated. Five thousand years ago people in Scotland were part of an international community of ideas that saw the rise of megalithic structures, and there is little reason to believe that we ever turned our back on the world. Why would we be different from other peoples and not have a mythology of our own? We know the Romans never affected us as they affected the English; we know now that Scotland is not descended from an Irish colony, no matter how central the Irish monk Columba may have been in the political development of our nation; we know the Picts did not need instruction on how to work stone in a country where carving had been taking place since the third millennium BC.

Our pre-Christian ancestors perhaps lacked all knowledge of writing, and our history over the past thousand years has seen a series of assaults on what little written history we had. Yet in the rich and vibrant traditions of our storytelling in both our major languages, in our ancient monuments and in our landscape there is much to be discovered. In the tales of the Cailleach, the place names referring to her and in so much related material, there is clear evidence of what can only be described as a mythology. Because much of the Lowlands have been continuously farmed since pre-Christian times, there is scant evidence there of how our ancestors lived. Yet in the stories and names they have left us in our landscapes, particularly in the hills and mountains, there is much for us to learn. It is only recently that the habit of devoting more than half our archaeological resources to digging up Roman remains has begun to wane. The Romans were here twice, each time for less than a generation. There are whole areas of Scotland that have hardly been investigated archaeologically. The archaeologists know what they are looking for when they dig up a Roman signal station or camp, but how many Roman nails do we need? Much work on the Picts is devoted to early Christian sites because again we have models of comparison with Christian communities elsewhere.

We need to look to ourselves to find our own answers as to who we are and where we come from. Suggesting a belief system structured around a bi-polar goddess linked to hundreds of sites throughout Scotland and surviving within the interlinked linguistic traditions of our land might be a place to start. Looking at extant material like the Gododdin compared to what we know of the poetical traditions of the Gaelic-speaking Highland tribes might be another. Out traditions have survived and today storytelling is resurgent. We should pay attention to our own, old tales for there is much to learn there.

Further Reading

BRADLEY, R., *An Archaeology of Natural Places* 2000

BRIGGS, K.M., *British Folk Tales and Legends : A Sampler* 1977

BRUFORD, D. and MacDONALD, D.A., *Scottish Traditional Tales* 1994

CAMERON, I.A., *Highland Chapbook* 1928

CAMPBELL, J.G., *Popular Tales of the West Highlands* 2 vols (reprint) 1994
More West Highland Tales 2 vols (reprint) 1994

DOUGLAS, S., *The King of the Black Art and Other Folk Tales* 1987

GREWAR, D., *The Story of Glenisla* 1926

HOPE, A.A., *Midsummer Eve's Dream* 1970

JERVISE, A., *Memorials of Angus and the Mearns* 1861
The Land of the Lindsays 1882

LEODHAS, SORCHE NIC, *Thistle and Thyme* 1962

LOCHHEAD, MARION, *The Battle of the Birds* 1981
Magic and Witchcraft of the Borders 1984

MacGREGOR, A.A., *The Peat Fire Flame* 1947

MacKENZIE, D.A., *Scottish Folk Lore and Folk Life* 1938

MCHARDY, S., *The Quest for the Nine Maidens* 2003

MCNEILL, F. MARIAN, *The Silver Bough* 4 vols (reprint) 1990

MCOWAN, R., *Magic Mountains* 1996

MARSHALL, W., *Historic Scenes in Perthshire* 1879

MILLER, T.D., *Tales of a Highland Parish* 1929

RITCHIE, J., *The Pageant of Moray* 1932

ROSS, A., *The Folklore of the Scottish Highlands* 1976

SIMPSON, E.B., *Folklore of Lowland Scotland* 1976

SWIRE, O., *The Highlands and their Legends* 1963
The Inner Hebrides and their Legends 1964
The Outer Hebrides and their Legends 1966

TEMPERLEY, A., *Tales of Galloway* 1979

WATSON, W.J., *The Celtic Placenames of Scotland* (reprint) 1993

WILLIAMSON, DUNCAN & LINDA, *The Thorn in the King's Foot* 1987

WILKIE, J., *Bygone Fife* 1937

WILSON, BARBARA K., *Scottish Folk-tales and Legends* 1954

Some other books published by **LUATH** PRESS

A New History of the Picts

Stuart McHardy
ISBN: 978-1-906817-70-1 PBK £8.99

The Picts hold a special place in the Scottish mind-set – a mysterious race of painted warriors, leaving behind imposing standing stones and not much more. Stuart McHardy challenges these long-held historical assumptions. He aims to get to the truth of who the Picts really were, and what their influence has been on Scotland's past and present.

McHardy demonstrates that rather than being some historical group of outsiders, or mysterious invaders, the Picts were in fact the indigenous people of Scotland and the most significant of our tribal ancestors. The Picts were not wiped out in battle, but gradually integrated with the Scots to form Alba. Their descendants walk our streets today.

Written and arranged in a way that is both accessible and scholarly, this is an excellent addition to the growing body of work on the Picts.
THE COURIER

Pagan Symbols of the Picts

Stuart McHardy
ISBN: 978-1-908373-14-4 HBK £14.99

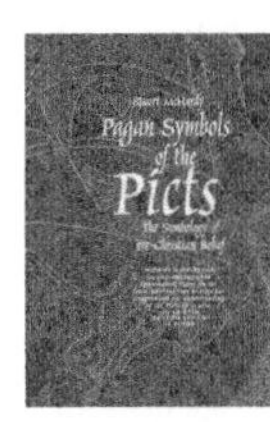

The Pagan Symbols of the Picts offers a fresh perspective on the importance of art, symbolism and the Picts in Scotland's cultural history. By looking beyond historical written accounts from Roman, Irish and Northumbrian sources, Stuart McHardy challenges traditional interpretations of Pictish stone art. Neither commemorative monuments nor an early alphabet, he instead explores their binary existence; as examples of larger shared beliefs in a linguistically and politically diverse landscape, and as objects of a very local genesis and influence. *The Pagan Symbols of the Picts* reveals not only the significance of Pictish symbology in the course of everyday life, but its place in the larger history of the Picts in Scotland and beyond.

Examining the temporal and geographic, the cultural and mythical, the artistic and oral, Stuart McHardy paints a vivid and diverse picture of Pictish Scotland.

The Quest for the Nine Maidens

Stuart McHardy

ISBN: 978-0-946487-66-0 HB £16.99

When Arthur was conveyed to Avalon they were there. When Odin summoned warriors to Valhalla they were there. When the Greek god Apollo was worshipped on mountaintops they were there. When Brendan came to the Island of Women they were there. Cerridwen's cauldron of inspiration was tended by them and Peredur received his arms from them. They are found in Pictland, Wales, Ireland, Iceland, Gaul, Greece, Africa and possibly as far a field as South America and Oceania.

They are the Nine Maidens, pagan priest-esses involved in the worship of the Mother Goddess. From Stone Age rituals to the 20th century, the Nine Maidens come in many forms. Muses, Maenads, valkyries and druidesses all associated with a single male. Weather – workers, shape – shifters, diviners and healers, the Nine Maidens are linked to the Old Religion over much of our planet. In this book Stuart McHardy has traced similar groups of Nine Maidens, throughout the ancient Celtic and Germanic world and far beyond, from Christian and pagan sources. In his search he begins to uncover one of the most ancient and widespread institutions of human society.

The Quest for Arthur

Stuart McHardy

ISBN 978-1-842820-12-4 HB £16.99

King Arthur of Camelot and the Knights of the Round Table are enduring romantic figures. A national hero for the Bretons, the Welsh and the English alike Arthur is a potent figure for many. This quest leads to a radical new inter-pretation of the ancient myth.

Historian, storyteller and folklorist Stuart McHardy believes he has uncovered the origins of this inspirational figure, the true Arthur. He incorporates knowledge of folklore and placename studies with an archaeological understanding of the 6th century.

Combining knowledge of the earliest records and histories of Arthur with an awareness of the importance of oral traditions, this quest leads to the discovery that the enigmatic origins of Arthur lie not in Brittany or England or Wales. Instead they lie in that magic land the ancient Welsh called *Y Gogledd*, the North; the North of Britain which we now call Scotland.

Edinburgh and Leith Pub Guide

Stuart McHardy

ISBN 978-1-906307-80-6 PB £4.95

You might be in Edinburgh to explore the closes and wynds of one of Europe's most beautiful cities, to sample the finest Scotch whiskies and to discover a rich Celtic heritage of traditional music and story-telling. Or you might be in Leith to get blootered. Either way, this is the guide for you.

Stuart McHardy has dragged his tired old frame around over two hundred pubs – all in the name of research, of course. Alongside drinking numerous pints, he has managed to compile enough historical anecdotes and practical information to allow anyone with a sturdy liver to follow in his footsteps.

Although Stuart unashamedly gives top marks to his favourite haunts, he rates most highly those pubs that are original, distinctive and cater to the needs of their clientele. Be it domino league or play-station league, pina colada or a pint of heavy, filled foccacia or mince and tatties, Stuart has found a decent pub that does it.

Scots Poems to be Read Aloud

Collectit an wi an innin by
Stuart McHardy
ISBN 978-0-946487-81-3 PBK £5.00

This is a book to encourage the traditional Scottish ceilidh of song and recitation.

This personal collection of well-known and not-so-well-known Scots poems to read aloud includes great works of art and simple pieces of questionable 'literary merit'.

For those who love poetry it's a wonderful anthology to have to hand, and for all those people who do not normally read poetry this collection is for you.

Scots Poems to be Read Aloud is pure entertainment – at home, on a stag or a hen night, Hogmanay, Burns Night, in fact any party night.
SUNDAY POST

The Supernatural Highlands

Francis Thompson
ISBN 978-0-946487-31-8 PBK £8.99

An authoritative exploration of the other-world of the Highlander, happenings and beings hitherto thought to be outwith the ordinary forces of nature. A simple introduction to the way of life of rural Highland and Island communities, this new edition weaves a path through second sight, the evil eye, witchcraft, ghosts, fairies and other supernatural beings, offering new sight-lines on areas of belief once dismissed as folklore and superstition.

This well-researched little book is written by someone who takes very seriously the ancient continuity of Gaelic culture, and asks us to keep an open mind about second sight, or the power of magic.
SCOTLAND ON SUNDAY

The Supernatural Highlands *is a substantive and thoughtful book and as such a valuable addition to the popular history of Scotland.*
THIS SCOTLAND

Luath Storyteller: Highland Myths & Legends

George W. Macpherson
ISBN 978-0-1-842820-64-3 PBK £5.00

The mythical, the legendary, the true… This is the stuff of stories and storytellers, the stuff of an age-old tradition in almost every country in the world, and none more so than Scotland. Celtic heroes, Fairies, Druids, Selkies, Sea horses, Magicians, Giants, Viking invaders; all feature in this collection of traditional Scottish tales, the like of which were told round camp fires centuries ago, and are still told today.

George W. Macpherson has dipped into his phenomenal repertoire of tales to compile this diverse collection of traditional stories, designed to be read aloud. Each has been passed from generation to generation, some are two and a half thousand years old.

From the Celtic legends of Cuchullin and Fionn to the mythical tales of seal-people and magicians these stories have a timeless quality. Often, strands of the stories will interweave and cross over, building a delicate tapestry of Scotland as a mystical, enchanted land.

The result is vivid and impressive, conveying the tragic dignity of the ancient warrior, or the devoted love of the seal woman and her fisher mate. The personalities and circumstances of people long gone are brought fully to life by the power of the storyteller's words. The ancestors take form before us in the visual imagination.

Dr Donald Smith, THE SCOTTISH STORY-TELLING CENTRE

one of Scotland's best storytellers
WESTDEUTSCHER RUNDFUNK KOHN

This is your genuine article
Mark Fisher, THE LIST

Legend and myth join with humour and gentle wit to create a special magic
Joy Hendry, SCOTSMAN

Luath Press Limited

committed to publishing well written books worth reading

LUATH PRESS takes its name from Robert Burns, whose little collie Luath (*Gael.*, swift or nimble) tripped up Jean Armour at a wedding and gave him the chance to speak to the woman who was to be his wife and the abiding love of his life. Burns called one of *The Twa Dogs* Luath after Cuchullin's hunting dog in *Ossian's Fingal*. Luath Press was established in 1981 in the heart of Burns country, and is now based a few steps up the road from Burns' first lodgings on Edinburgh's Royal Mile.
Luath offers you distinctive writing with a hint of unexpected pleasures.

Most bookshops in the UK, the US, Canada, Australia, New Zealand and parts of Europe either carry our books in stock or can order them for you. To order direct from us, please send a £sterling cheque, postal order, international money order or your credit card details (number, address of cardholder and expiry date) to us at the address below. Please add post and packing as follows: UK – £1.00 per delivery address; overseas surface mail – £2.50 per delivery address; overseas airmail – £3.50 for the first book to each delivery address, plus £1.00 for each additional book by airmail to the same address. If your order is a gift, we will happily enclose your card or message at no extra charge.

ILLUSTRATION: IAN KELLAS

Luath Press Limited
543/2 Castlehill
The Royal Mile
Edinburgh EH1 2ND
Scotland

Telephone: 0131 225 4326 (24 hours)
Fax: 0131 225 4324
email: sales@luath.co.uk
Website: www.luath.co.uk